Her book provides an easy to read, informative introduction to a wide variety of legal issues. It is both an excellent starting place for those concerned with a particular issue and an entertaining reference book on how the law affects us on a day-to-day basis.

> – from the foreword of Justice R. James Williams,
> Supreme Court of Nova Scotia (Family Division)

Very interesting! . . . Using a plainspoken style, *Everything You Wanted to Know, But Couldn't Afford to Ask* is a helpful and accessible tool for Nova Scotians puzzling over basic questions about the law and legal process.

> – Anne S. Derrick, Q.C.

I am most impressed. I found this information to be interesting, accurate and practical. I am sure many Nova Scotians will be attracted to this excellent piece of work.

> – Kevin Coady, Q.C.
> Vice President (2nd) Nova Scotia Barristers' Society

This book is a must read. With wit and charming anecdote, Lisa Teryl opens the lawyer's door, invites us in, demystifies the jargon, and educates us to the countless questions about the law that continually crop up in our daily lives.

> – Augusta (Lisa's mother)

A gift is to have two parents
give an ocean of love and support.

A blessing is to reach for a star
and have two brothers and a sister
scramble to hold the ladder.

A delight is to have both Michel/les and Joy
share a path along the way.

Thank you, also, to Lesley for providing the opportunity,
to Jen for sharing the work,
and to Kim for watching out for me.

Nova Scotia Law:

Everything You Wanted To Know, But Couldn't Afford To Ask

Lisa Teryl

Pottersfield Press, Lawrencetown Beach, Nova Scotia

National Library of Canada Cataloguing in Publication
Teryl, Lisa
Nova Scotia law: everything you wanted to know, but couldn't afford to ask /Lisa Teryl.
        ISBN 1-895900-53-0
        1. Law — Nova Scotia — Miscellanea. I. Title.
KEN7574.T47 2002   349.716   C2002-903592-9

Book cover design by Black Dog Advertising, Bedford, Nova Scotia

Pottersfield Press acknowledges the ongoing support of the Nova Scotia Department of Tourism and Culture, Cultural Affairs Division. We acknowledge the support of the Canada Council for the Arts which last year invested $19.1 million in writing and publishing throughout Canada. We also acknowledge the finanacial support of the Government of Canada through the Book Publishing Industry Development Program for our publishing activities.

Pottersfield Press
83 Leslie Road
East Lawrencetown
 Nova Scotia, Canada B2Z 1P8
Web site: www.pottersfieldpress.com
To order, phone 1-800-NIMBUS9 (1-800-646-2879)
Printed in Canada

Contents

Foreword

Almost everything we do is affected by the law in some way. Making law more understandable and accessible to the public is an admirable and daunting task.

Lisa Teryl has, in this book, succeeded in just such an undertaking. Her book provides an easy to read, informative introduction to a wide variety of legal issues. It is both an excellent starting place for those concerned with a particular legal issue and an entertaining reference book on how the law affects us on a day-to-day basis.

It is not (and does not purport to be) a substitute for consulting with a lawyer if you have a specific legal issue or concern. It does, however, provide Nova Scotians with a "home legal reference book" that informs, clarifies and demystifies.

Justice R. James Williams
Supreme Court of Nova Scotia
(Family Division)

Preface

On a cold morning during the final days of flu season, looking up at the bedroom ceiling, it occurred to me that I could write a question/answer legal column for a newspaper. I wanted it to be a legal column that was easy to read, entertaining and informative.

In March 2000 the first of my legal advice columns rolled off the presses of the *Sunday Daily News*. Two years later, Lesley Choyce of Pottersfield Press picked up the spirit of the column and agreed that the body of work would make a great law reference book for Nova Scotians.

I have had important help with the column's legal editing. I thank Kim Richardson, who is one of the smartest and nicest lawyers I know; my brother, Shawn Scott, for his assistance researching some of the finer legal points and his cartooning talents; and my good friend Michele Cleary for her general comments and support (imagine, another smart and nice lawyer!). My thanks also to Jean Webb, lawyer and tenancy court adjudicator, who gave the Tenants, Landlords and -Ladies chapter a final edit. I also thank freelance writer extraordinaire Michelle Thomason who assisted with general editing as well as the folks at the *Daily News*.

Finally, I would like to thank Justice R. James Williams of the Nova Scotia Supreme Court (Family Division) for supporting this project by providing the book's foreword, and Anne Derrick, Q.C., and Kevin Coady, Q.C., for reviewing the manuscript and providing helpful comments.

Please contact a lawyer to review your particular facts before acting on your legal problem. This book is providing legal information and is not to be relied upon as legal advice since situations and circumstances vary and the law may have changed since the date of this publication.

Lisa Teryl, August 2002
Teryl Scott, Lawyers inc.
1254 Bedford Highway
Halifax,
Nova Scotia, B4A 1C6
1-877-692-1366
lisa@terylscott.com
www.terylscott.com

What do you mean you want to speak to a lawyer?

Civil Disputes

Car Warranties

DEAR LISA

I just bought a used car from a dealer who told me before I bought it that it was in "great shape." Four days later the muffler fell off and it cost me $400 to repair it. I feel I was ripped off. What can I do?

SMELLING A LEMON

DEAR SMELLING A LEMON

It depends on the representations made at the time you bought the car and whether there was a warranty. Did the dealer specifically tell you the muffler was fine (or just the car in general)? Are there any written warranties about the muffler?

The Sale of Goods Act also creates an implied warranty that the vehicle should be "fit for the purpose for which it was sold." But in reality, unless you answer yes to one of the above questions, you will probably not get your money back. Small Claims Court would be the court to hear your claim.

DEAR LISA

I bought a car three years ago and it had a 4-year/80,000-kilometre bumper-to-bumper warranty. I took the car in for a full check up at 81,000 kilometres. They found a problem with the engine. The dealer says he won't cover it under warranty because I am 1,000 kilometres over the limit. Is this true?

WARRANTY WORRIER

DEAR WARRANTY WORRIER

The manufacturer's warranty usually expires at exactly 80,000 kilometres or after four years, whichever comes first. In your case, it appears you are 1,000 kilometres too late to be covered by the contract. It is like your birthday: when you turn 20 years old, you are 20, not 19.

DEAR LISA

I recently bought a car with an extended warranty from a used car dealer. Something was wrong with my transmission that should have been covered by the warranty, but the dealer will not cover it. He says because I had my oil changed after 8,500 kilometres instead of 8,000 kilometres, I didn't follow the instructions and therefore my warranty is invalid. Is that true? Where does the warranty end and the doormat begin?

SUSPICIOUS

DEAR SUSPICIOUS

The warranty has limits, but not exactly the way the dealer told you. Unless the dealer can prove that the extra 500 kilometres without the new oil change materially affected your transmission, he will likely have to cover the defect.

Case law says if there is "substantial performance" of the warranty terms by you, the court will force the dealer to comply with the warranty. You do not have to be perfect in completing the warranty terms.

DEAR LISA

My 3-year-old car has a problem with its transmission. The manufacturer will not cover the problem. Is Small Claims Court my only inexpensive option?

TAKING STOCK OF MY OPTIONS

DEAR OPTIONS

The Better Business Bureau promotes an organization called the Canadian Motor Vehicle Arbitration Plan (CAMVAP)(1-800-207-0685), created to arbitrate disputes between manufacturers and vehicle owners.

Your car must be less than four years old and have traveled less than 160,000 kilometres. Most of the major manufacturers (19) have agreed to participate. The hearing is free of charge and is an alternative to court. The decision is binding on both parties and can only be appealed under certain circumstances. Similar to Small Claims Court, the entire process takes about two months.

Home Oil Leaks

DEAR LISA

I recently bought a house that is now an environmental disaster. Apparently there was an old oil tank buried in my yard. The statement of disclosure from the seller, though, said there were no buried oil tanks. I now have oil leaking into my well. My insurance company has denied coverage. My neighbour tells me it was buried by the previous owner to the one I bought from. Who can I sue?

LEAKS AND LIES

DEAR LEAKS AND LIES

Sue the person who sold you the house for breach of the disclosure agreement. Your success depends on whether the misrepresentation was intentional, negligent, or innocent. If the owner knew about it (intentional) or should have known about it (negligent), you have a good case. If this owner did not know about the tank (innocent) because she was relying on a disclosure statement from the owner who buried the tank, this makes your case more difficult. You may also want to consider whether this was something your house inspector (if you hired one) should have noticed when you bought the house.

DEAR LISA

The oil tank in my basement hasn't leaked yet but if it does, will my insurance company cover any damage to the things in my basement? My policy doesn't appear to mention it.

LEAK ALERT

DEAR ALERT

Unfortunately, many house insurance policies do not explicitly say whether they cover this loss in your home. If you do not have this coverage explicitly stated in your policy, insurance companies take a wait (until the accident) and see (if they will cover you) approach. This policy interpretation, though, is not so helpful from the consumer point of view.

There are, however, companies (Portage La Prairie Mutual or Royal & Sunalliance, for example) that will state expressly in your insurance policy that they cover this loss. I recommend you shop around for better house insurance or ask your current insurer to confirm in writing whether or not they will cover this loss.

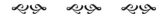

Debts/Collection

DEAR LISA

I want to declare bankruptcy to eliminate my personal income tax debt. Will bankruptcy do this for me?

DITCHING THE LOAD

DEAR DITCHING

It depends. You can eliminate income tax debt if it is not in the form of a judgment on your home. If the tax debt is registered at the Registry of Deeds, the government debt will survive the bankruptcy.

This exception only applies to income tax judgments already at the Registry. If the tax debt is not yet a judgment when your bankruptcy is declared, the government cannot take any further action and your bankruptcy will become effective against their debt. Other non-income tax judgments against your home, however, would normally be eliminated by bankruptcy if you list them in your bankruptcy.

Be warned, however, that your creditors (including the government) have the right to object to the discharge of your bankruptcy. They can request a court to hold open your bankruptcy beyond the nine months that it usually takes to become automatically discharged. During this period of time, if you have the income to pay off some or all of these debts, you will be required to do so.

DEAR LISA

I am a co-signer of a debt for my boyfriend. Since he is the principal debtor, are we equally responsible for the debt?

JUST DOING A FAVOR

DEAR FAVOUR

Legally, you will be "jointly and severally" responsible for the debt. This means the bank can legally pursue either one of you. Furthermore, the bank can pursue you for all (as opposed to half) of the debt. You may want to avoid signing for his debts where possible, unless you are prepared to pay off his debts even after you part ways (should that happen).

DEAR LISA

The collection creditors are hounding me for payment on my delinquent credit card bills. They are threatening to sue me. What happens if they sue me and win?

DEEP IN DEBT

DEAR IN DEBT

Debt collectors threaten to sue often, but it is their least favorite way of trying to get the money. When they successfully sue you in court, they get a "judgment" against you for the amount of the debt. The rate of interest on this judgment debt drops from approximately 27 percent (credit card rates) to 5 percent (*Judicature Act*). With a judgment, these are some of the things a creditor can do:

- They can garnish your wages if they know where you work;

- After a year, they can take steps to sell your house to pay the debt, (but this rarely happens unless it is a mortgage debt and the bank, for example, forecloses);

- The judgment is registered at the Registry of Deeds and sits there quietly until you buy or sell a piece of property, at which time you must pay the debt.

The third option is what usually happens to small (under $5,000) credit card debts.

DEAR LISA

I just won a judgment at Small Claims Court for $1,000 against my contractor. How do I get the money out of him now?

SMELLING VICTORY

DEAR VICTORY

You will now need an execution order, which you get from the Small

Claims Court. With an execution order, information about the contractor's place of business and bank account numbers, you can go to the sheriff, who will attempt to enforce it. The sheriff can go to the contractor's place of business and take cash out of the till or take other valuable property. If they are employed, you can get a garnishment on their wages with the same execution order.

DEAR LISA

How can I collect a debt from someone who lives in Ontario? I loaned a former co-worker money when she was here in Nova Scotia.

MONEY OWED

DEAR MONEY OWED

If you cannot get her to pay voluntarily, you will need a court order. The Nova Scotian courts have jurisdiction to hear the claim since the debt contract originated here. But there are four steps to take:

- You must also have an Ontario court reconfirm this order before you can collect it in Ontario. The *Reciprocal Enforcement of Judgments Act* (Ont) (http://192.75.156.68/DBLaws/Statutes/English/90r05_e.htm) outlines how this is done and what criteria are required to get it registered in there.

- When you send the order to be confirmed in the Ontario court, you have to give the person notice of your application to register the order in Ontario if
  - a) they were not previously personally served for the Nova Scotia hearing, and
  - b) they did not attend it.

- Then, you have the Ontario order personally served on the defendant within 30 days of the court issuing it. This provides her with notice of the Ontario order so she can contest it if she has not already.

- Finally, contact the sheriff nearest to the person in Ontario and have them attempt to collect the debt.

DEAR LISA

My former son-in-law borrowed $2,000 from me to buy an ATV, which he still drives. I loaned him the money three years ago. Since my daughter broke up with him, he hasn't paid me anything (although he should have paid me back by now). I heard he has a personal injury settlement coming his way this year and it is worth a lot. Can I get some of this settlement money to pay the debt?

BANKER-IN-LAW

DEAR BANKER

There are at least two ways to ensure you get your money from his settlement funds.

You can ask him to sign an "irrevocable direction to pay," which his personal-injury lawyer can draw up. If he agrees to sign this document, his lawyer must pay you before he pays your former son-in-law any of the proceeds from the settlement. Should your son-in-law change his mind about paying you after he signed the direction to pay, the lawyer is nonetheless obligated to pay you.

In the event your former son-in-law will not sign this direction to pay, you should immediately take the debt to Small Claims Court. When you get a judgment at Small Claims Court, you can serve it and a "third party notice" to his lawyer, who is then obligated to pay you before your former son-in-law.

DEAR LISA

My future son-in-law is being bothered by a collection agency about his student loan. They made him send money orders by priority post which costs more. He has reached the point where he hates to answer his phone. He really needs some advice. Hope you can help.

JUST TRYING TO HELP

DEAR TRYING

Your son-in-law is never obligated to pay debts – delinquent or otherwise – by money order or priority post, unless stipulated in the original contract. These are added expenses not provided for by the contract.

Court action is the worst a creditor can threaten. Some unethical collection agents can be abusive in their tone, which can be much worse than a trip to Small Claims Court (for debts under $10,000). The conduct of collection agents and agencies must conform to the *Collection Agencies Act* (s. 20). I have discussed this earlier, but if a judgment is taken out against your son, the interest rate on the debt drops to 5 percent. I strongly recommend that your son-in-law consider getting an unlisted number. He ultimately chooses how and when he wishes to pay back his debts if a judgment has not been obtained from the court.

DEAR LISA

I have another question on collection agents. My son-in-law is still having troubles. The collection agency wants his bank account number so they can take payments from his account. Can they do this without him signing something?

STILL JUST TRYING TO HELP

DEAR STILL TRYING

No, the bank must have written authorization from your son-in-law. If he chooses to set up automatic debit to pay back the loan (although he is not obligated to do so), and then decides to cancel it, he must give the bank written notice of the date he wishes the cancellation to take effect. He should date this cancellation letter and keep a copy for his records. Should they proceed to debit his account after he cancelled it, the bank must reimburse him for it.

DEAR LISA

I am pulling out my hair with credit cards debts and personal loan payments to the bank. How does the Orderly Payment of Debts program work? Is there any court involved?

BALDLY GOING WHERE NO ONE HAS GONE BEFORE

DEAR BALDLY

Live long and prosper. Yes, there is court involved in the form of a court order. You can contact a counsellor of this program at Service Nova Scotia and Municipal Relations (1-800-670-4357). She will review your entire debt situation with the goal of having you repay all of your debt within three to five years. If this repayment time-line is possible, she then gets a court order to consolidate your debts (except your mortgage and possibly other secured debts). Your consolidated debts must be less than $75,000.

After the court order, you have only a single monthly payment, which you pay to the Orderly Payment of Debts program. They distribute the money to your creditors for you. If you miss in total three months of payments while in the program, the creditors can once again collect directly from you.

The incentive to take this option is that the interest rate on your debts drops to a mere 5 percent simple annual interest. Such a low interest rate is similar to a mortgage rate and will allow you to pay down the debt more quickly. Another benefit is creditors cannot take further legal action against you, such as garnishing your wages while you are with the program.

The downside is you cannot get any more credit while in the program and it negatively affects your credit rating. Although, if any of your debts have gone to collection, your credit has already been affected.

DEAR LISA

I have a gambling addiction that I developed after my daughter died in a car accident. I wrote a bad cheque on my bank account for $3,000; I knew the money wasn't in the account. The collection department for the bank worked out a pay-back schedule and I have only been able to make a few payments. The collector called me the other day and left a message on my machine threatening to contact the RCMP if I didn't bring my payments up to date. What can I do?

RECOVERING BUT WORRIED

DEAR RECOVERING

Keep the message on your machine as evidence. You may need it in your criminal defence. Although the bank may call the police, it is doubtful that you would be successfully prosecuted for fraud because of how the collection agent handled the matter. The police may be reluctant to now get involved because the criminal courts have considered it an "abuse of process" when a debtor (the bank) uses the criminal law as a stick to collect debt.

Even if the police lay a charge, if this message machine tape is presented to the court, the criminal prosecution would probably be stayed (permanently stopped). You would be then free to go, with no trial or conviction and no possibility of further prosecution on the matter. The bank, though, can still sue you for the $3,000 judgment.

Breach of Privacy

DEAR LISA

I have a terminal illness which required me to leave work and go on disability. I received disability insurance for about two years, which was then reduced when I applied for, and received, Canada Pension Plan disability benefits. My disability insurer wanted me to sign a waiver of confidentiality to allow them access to my CPP information. I refused to sign it because it is personal information.

I just found out from my insurance company that they obtained the information from CPP even though I didn't sign the release of information (the waiver). To get the information, the insurance company gave CPP, over the phone, my SIN number, birth date and name. Can they do this legally?

WAIVING THE FINGER

DEAR WAIVING

No, your CPP information is not to be disclosed to anyone unless you sign a waiver. Unless your insurance company can show they obtained your consent or they had a court order to get it, it appears they have intentionally breached your privacy by posing as you over the phone.

You may want to contact the police and/or the Superintendent of Insurance (902-424-6331) to file a complaint. Suing civilly could be more difficult because breach of privacy between individuals (as opposed to government breaches) is not a well developed area of law.

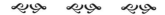

DEAR LISA

What are the laws or rights of individuals on recording conversations? Can a person secretly tape my in-person conversation with them? Isn't that a violation of my privacy?

FEELING DUPED

DEAR FEELING DUPED

Yes, they can tape your conversation. Although it may feel like a violation of your privacy, it is not illegal. The *Criminal Code* only makes it an offence to tape private conversations if none of the parties in the conversation consent to the recording. For example, it is illegal to bug someone's phone when neither that person nor the caller knows of the bug. There is a maximum punishment of five years for this type of eavesdropping.

If there is any police involvement, however, (whether there is consent from a party or not) there generally has to be an authorization from a judge to listen in or record the communications. If they do not have this authorization, the police may not be able to use the information as evidence at trial. This lack of authorization by police would be considered a breach of a person's right to privacy under the Charter (s.8).

The Charter does not protect your privacy rights when breached by the other person, though, because she is not an agent of the state. The Charter only restricts government actions, not private relations between parties. The provincial and federal legislative human rights codes regulate the private sector. The Nova Scotia *Human Rights Act*, though, does not explicitly protect the right to privacy.

Employment Contracts

DEAR LISA

I was recently terminated from my employment after 15 years of service. The company manager claimed that I stole funds from the company. She even told other employees this was why I was terminated. There was a theft problem at work, but I didn't steal anything. I am finding it difficult now to find work. What can I do?

FALSELY ACCUSED

DEAR FALSELY

You can sue for wrongful dismissal and defamation. If the court agrees that you did not steal anything and therefore there was no just cause to dismiss you, you may be entitled to "bad faith" damages. The Nova Scotia Supreme Court (*Musgrave v. Levesque Securities*) awarded twice the amount of damages the plaintiff normally would have received for being wrongfully dismissed in a situation where the employer was unduly harsh in the manner of dismissal, including slandering the employee to other employees.

Generally, damages are about one month's pay (even this amount fluctuates depending on certain factors) for every year you have worked for your employer. The Supreme Court of Canada (*Wallace v. United Grain Growers*) defines bad faith to include the following actions by an employer: maintaining a wrongful accusation of theft; refusing to provide a reference letter; reassuring an employee that a position will be found while planning for her termination; and terminating an employee while on disability leave.

(My thanks to Scott Sterns at Jamieson Sterns for his research and comments.)

DEAR LISA

Why can I be sued for theft by my employer if I was acquitted of the criminal charges?

HAVING A BAD WEEK

DEAR BAD WEEK

For the criminal charges, the Crown has a very high burden to prove your guilt: beyond a reasonable doubt or a moral certainty that you committed the theft. In civil court, though, your employer only has to prove theft "on a balance of probabilities," that is, more likely than not you committed the theft. This is a standard much lower than the Crown's.

When you were acquitted at criminal trial, it did not mean you were not at fault. It only means the Crown did not prove your guilt beyond a reasonable doubt. O.J. Simpson's experience illustrates how you can win in criminal court and lose on the same issue in civil court.

House Insurance Coverage

DEAR LISA

I went to Winnipeg for Christmas to visit my family. When I returned to my apartment, I found my fridge and freezer had malfunctioned. All the food, which was worth over $200, had spoiled. Will my personal property/content insurance cover this loss? If so, does a deductible apply? My insurance broker thought I would have to pay a deductible.

SPOILED ROTTEN

DEAR SPOILED

Your insurance policy is written in (fairly) plain English. I highly recommend reading it, even if you are only contemplating making a claim. In this case, your insurance broker may be mistaken that you have to pay the deductible. There are different levels of coverage depending on the price you pay for the policy. Some personal property insurance policies cover food losses up to $1,000 when caused by fridge breakdowns or power failures. Furthermore, you may have coverage where there is no deductible to pay. Your policy may pay for 100 percent of your losses.

Then there's the old story
involving the theft of some chickens...

Criminal

Harassment/Peace Bonds

DEAR LISA

My 8-year-old son is being bullied at school by one child in particular. My son tells me this other child, who is nine years old, will intentionally trip him in the hallway and call him demeaning names. I have contacted the school with my concerns that the abuse is escalating. My normally happy child has become quite sullen and moody because of these problems. What can I do? Shouldn't this be a criminal offence?

FEELING HELPLESS TO A BULLY

DEAR FEELING HELPLESS

Since the offending child is under the age of 12, she or he is not covered by the *Criminal Code*. Philosophically, lawmakers are reluctant to lower the age because the criminal law is a big stick to curb a child's behaviour. There are usually other more appropriate options available, like counseling and/or providing other support and better parental discipline.

My sister Chris Augusta-Scott, a psychologist (Candidate Register) at the Fall River Family Practice and a former principal with Halifax Regional School Board, offers these suggestions:

- Make a verbal complaint to the teacher. Then if the bullying does not stop, follow it up with a phone call or a letter to the principal stating your concerns.
- Ask for a meeting between the principal or vice-principal to discuss your concerns. You may want to meet with the parents of the bully too.
- A school social worker may also be able to offer support for your child.
- Check the Internet for web sites on bullying (www.askjeeves. com search word: bully). These sites offer strategies and helpful information about the problem.
- Many schools teach a curriculum which offers life skills to children, part of which is how to deal with bullies. Ask your son's teacher about these programs.
- The local police will often come to classrooms and talk about bullying. Halifax Regional Police also have a hotline for kids (902-490-7283) who are bullied or for kids who do not want to be a bully anymore.

Your son may need to talk to a child psychologist to get direct strategies for how to deal with his particular bully.

DEAR LISA

How do I get a peace bond against my ex-girlfriend?

PEACE NIC

DEAR PEACE NIC

Get the peace bond application form from your local Provincial Court.

The local police will arrange to give your ex-girlfriend the summons to court (for approximately $35). You both have to attend.

There are two court appearances usually required. The first one (called a "docket appearance") is to get a date for the full hearing in front of a judge (which is the second appearance). A full hearing is only required if your ex-girlfriend will not agree to be bound by the peace bond at the docket appearance.

Successfully getting a peace bond against your ex-girlfriend does not mean she gets a criminal record. It is just a formal promise to stay away from you. If she breaks that promise, she can then be charged with breaching a peace bond. If convicted, she would then have a criminal record.

Lawyers generally charge from $500 to $2,500 to represent you at such a hearing, depending on the complexity of the matter and time involved. You may also represent yourself.

DEAR LISA

My ex-piano teacher won't leave me alone. He keeps following me around and making phone calls. I'm scared. What can I do?

FEELING STALKED

DEAR FEELING STALKED

You could get a peace bond (as discussed above) or you can call the police. If you are feeling threatened, the police can lay a "criminal harassment" charge. Unlike the granting of a peace bond, your stalker will get a conviction if successfully prosecuted. To get a conviction, the Crown must prove your ex-piano teacher caused you to "reasonably fear" for your safety or the safety of anyone known to you (s.264, *Criminal Code*).

DEAR LISA

I am black and drive a nice car which I inherited from my mother. The police keep stopping me and searching my car for no good reason, although they say they are looking for drugs. When can a police officer search my car?

SEARCHED AND BOTHERED

DEAR BOTHERED

Police officers are allowed to search your car if they have "reasonable and probable grounds to believe there has been an offence committed." For example, if they smell alcohol or marijuana in a person's car, this would be reasonable and probable grounds to search the car for these items. If the police, however, do not have the grounds to stop you in the first place, any evidence found in the search can sometimes be excluded at trial.

If you think you are being illegally searched (i.e., they do not have any grounds for the search), take the name of the officer who stopped you and register a complaint with the Nova Scotia Human Rights Commission (1-877-269-7699) and/or your local Police Commission (Halifax: 424-3246).

Criminal Court Procedure

DEAR LISA

I had a friend who was charged with a crime and her lawyer told her not to testify. Why would an accused person choose not to testify at her own trial?

SPEAKING UP

DEAR SPEAKING UP

Although there are many reasons why a defence attorney would not want their client to take the stand, the most common reason is because their client has a criminal record. The Crown attorney is not permitted to reveal the accused has a criminal record unless the accused takes the stand. If your friend did testify, the Crown could have then asked her questions about previous criminal convictions.

On occasion, I recommend accused clients not take the stand even though they do not have a criminal record. In such cases, the Crown may not have presented enough evidence to prove beyond a reasonable doubt the offence, or the client will make an unfavorable impression on the judge or jury even though they do not have a criminal record.

DEAR LISA

Can the guy who assaulted me be found guilty if it is only my word against his? I was sexually assaulted and I am a witness at the upcoming trial.

LOOKING FOR A GOOD WORD

DEAR LOOKING

The Crown attorney might not call any further evidence other than your word. To get a conviction, however, the Crown must convince the judge that you are to be believed rather than the accused. It must be shown beyond a reasonable doubt that your version of events on all the elements of the offence is to be believed.

Prior to 1985, though, the *Criminal Code* required corroborating evidence such as a witness or physical evidence to support a woman's testimony of rape (as it was called then). Historically, legislators considered that a woman's testimony on its own could not convict an accused even if the judge believed the woman and thought the man a liar. Also, her complaint had to be recently laid with the police or a bad inference could be made against her credibility. Fortunately, times change and the *Criminal Code* now considers a woman's word as good as a man's.

DEAR LISA

My son has been charged with theft over $5,000 for stealing a car. What is the difference between a summary and an indictable offence? The Crown says they are proceeding "indictably."

WORRIED SICK

DEAR WORRIED SICK

A summary offence is an offence that carries a lesser maximum punishment than those prosecuted by indictment. They are called "summary" because the trial process is abbreviated – there is no right to a preliminary hearing or a jury. Some offences can proceed either way and are called hybrid offences. The Crown attorney has the final say whether to proceed summarily or indictably with these offences. The seriousness of the facts surrounding the offence and prior convictions of the offender are considerations in deciding which way the Crown will go.

Just because the Crown has decided to proceed indictably does not mean the judge will sentence your son more harshly (should he be convicted). The facts of the case and your son's background would be the most important considerations for his sentencing.

DEAR LISA

How can criminal defence lawyers in good conscience represent murderers and rapists?

MORALLY SEARCHING

DEAR SEARCHING

Criminal defence lawyers are the "watchdogs of the state." They have an important role protecting basic human rights within the criminal justice system. Allowing criminal defence lawyers to enforce due process is a distinguishing feature between our state and an abusive police state. If the state has the proper checks and balances (i.e., produces fair results), I do not mind representing offenders and supporting them through the process. It is like having a delinquent brother whose acts you don't agree with, but you still want him to be treated fairly.

DEAR LISA

I was robbed while clerking at a convenience store. The guy threatened me with a knife but I wasn't injured. The police officer told me this was his first offence. Is he going down the river?

LOOKING FOR RIVERSIDE SEATING

DEAR LOOKING

Yes. The courts particularly abhor robberies of homes and small businesses. If convicted, your robber can expect one to two years, minimum, down the river to Springhill or Dorchester or a similar conditional sentence. A conditional sentence allows a person to serve the jail time at home with a strict curfew. If they breach their conditions, they serve the remainder of their sentence in jail.

DEAR LISA

I was arrested for shoplifting recently. The police officer said I had a right to a lawyer, but didn't really elaborate. What exactly are they supposed to tell me, and what happens if they don't say what they are supposed to?

INNOCENT UNTIL PROVEN GUILTY

DEAR INNOCENT

Recent Nova Scotia Court of Appeal cases (*R. v. Chisholm* and *R. v. Nickerson*) have confirmed strict guidelines on what information the police must provide you about your right to a lawyer. The police must tell you all of the following when they arrest you:

- you can speak to a lawyer immediately;
- there is duty counsel available 24 hours per day to provide temporary legal advice;
- duty counsel is available free of charge regardless of your income;
- there is a toll free number if you wish you speak to duty counsel, which the police officer should offer to give you;
- Legal Aid is also available for long term legal representation, if you cannot afford a lawyer.

If you were not provided with all of this information, among other things, you can ask the judge to stay (permanently stop) the charges or exclude important evidence (due to a s.10(b) Charter violation).

DEAR LISA

I had a fire in my apartment and my insurance company wants me to give a statement. I am worried because the police are also investigating whether the fire was arson. Do I have to give a statement to my insurance company? Can it be used against me in a criminal trial if the police charge me?

FIREBUGGED

DEAR FIREBUGGED

Yes, your insurance contract requires you to give a statement to your insurance adjuster if you want them to cover your losses. If you choose to give one, I recommend you have a lawyer present and that you begin the statement by saying: "I only give this statement because I am obligated to do so under the *Insurance Act*."

If you then have a criminal trial, you can ask the court not to allow the insurance statement to be used as evidence against you. The court has the power to exclude the statement using section 7 of the Charter, which protects your right not to incriminate yourself (i.e., the right to remain silent). Voluntary incriminating statements, however, are generally not protected by the Charter. Saying you are obligated to give the insurance statement helps establish the statement as non-voluntary and therefore not useable at criminal trial.

Juries

DEAR LISA

I was subpoenaed for jury duty but I had already planned a bingo bus trip to Louisiana with my friends. Even though I would love to be a juror for a big trial, I don't want to miss my trip and lose my deposit. Do I have to go to court?

BUSTED FLAT

DEAR BUSTED

You may be still able to go on the bus trip if you apply to be excused from jury duty. The jury co-ordinator can excuse you because of "hardship or illness" or can put you off to a later date if it is "inconvenient" for you to show up on the date given in your summons. If, however, the jury co-ordinator refuses your application to be excused, you must show up at court. You can still ask the judge, though, to excuse you when you are first called into the courtroom.

You can also avoid duty if you fit within a class of persons disqualified from jury duty: for example, if you are a law student, police officer or court worker. The law courts can provide you with a full list.

If you fail to show up at court for jury duty and you did not have consent from the court to be absent, you could be arrested and fined up to $1,000.

In your case, you can probably at least get your jury duty deferred by the co-ordinator to the end of the month, after your bus trip. The co-ordinator will let you know by telephone if your application has been approved or denied.

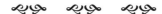

Hate Crimes

DEAR LISA

I was shocked to hear of the vandalism against our local Islamic mosque last weekend. Our church, which is Christian, is going to send a donation to show our support. Why hasn't the man who did the damage been charged with a hate crime?

FAITHFUL

DEAR FAITHFUL

I, too, was sad to hear of this attack on our Muslim community. There is no hate crime charge that would appear to apply to this situation. For example, there are charges for hate propaganda and incitement of hatred against identifiable groups, but these crimes have particular definitions and do not cover this situation. The *Criminal Code* (s.718.2), however, does allow a harsher sentence for a crime if there is "evidence that the offence was motivated by bias, prejudice or hate based on race, national or ethnic origin, language, colour, religion, sex, age, mental or physical disability, sexual orientation or any other similar factor."

In this case, if the man is convicted of property damage (mischief), he will face a maximum term of two years' imprisonment. The judge would consider aggravating factors, such as the attack being motivated by religious intolerance, and would probably give a harsher sentence than otherwise.

Criminal Record Checks

DEAR LISA

The last time I hired a salesperson, I belatedly found out he had a criminal record for fraud. How do I get a criminal record check on prospective employees?

ONCE ROBBED, TWICE SHY

DEAR ROBBED

Request the employee go to your local police station to fill out police forms confirming the employee has no criminal record. There is no fee for checks done with the RCMP, but there may be fees with the local police. You must have the employee's consent to have access to his or her record.

DEAR LISA

I have a Small Claims Court action against a customer who stole a stereo from my store. How do I get evidence of her criminal record into court? I know she has a criminal record for theft.

MATLOCK FOR A NIGHT

DEAR MATLOCK

You must subpoena a constable from the local police department for it. The constable attends the hearing and brings a print-out of her criminal record or the whole police file. They will require her full name and birth date (or her address may help if you do not have a birth date). There are further subpoena requirements:

- You must name a particular person on the subpoena, not just the "RCMP," for example;

- Send the subpoena down to the Small Claims Court to be issued (they confirm that there is actually a court hearing on the date specified in the subpoena);

- A copy of the court-issued subpoena and a small witness fee must then be personally served on the constable;

- The person serving the constable should be someone other than you. The server should not be a party to the action. There are professional "process servers" who also do this for about $50;

- Have the person who served the subpoena swear an affidavit confirming it was personally served;

- Bring the original affidavit and subpoena to court;

- Ask for an adjournment if, for some reason, the constable cannot attend.

Drug Offences

DEAR LISA

The police raided my house last night and I have been charged with possession of marijuana. I have no prior criminal convictions and they only found a couple of joints. If I am convicted, what type of sentence will I get?

NOT SO RELAXED

DEAR NOT SO RELAXED

The courts often impose a fine of $150 or more, depending upon the judge.

Prior to pleading guilty or not guilty, however, you can call the Crown attorney and ask if they would consider diverting you into "adult diversion." If you go this route, you would not have to go to court at all and you would avoid getting a criminal record. To be accepted into the program, you have to admit you committed the offence. The program may require you to do some community service (or co-operate in other ways).

If you have to go to court and are found guilty, you may ask for a conditional or an absolute discharge. A discharge would also mean you have no criminal conviction. The court does not have to grant you a discharge and it depends on various circumstances (for example, if a criminal conviction would affect your employment prospects, the judge may grant you a discharge).

Motor Vehicle Offences

DEAR LISA

A woman I know hit and injured a pedestrian a couple weeks ago. She panicked and did not stop at the accident. She turned herself in to police that night, after she calmed down. What kind of trouble is she in?

CURIOUS ACQUAINTANCE

DEAR CURIOUS

This woman has committed an offence under both the *Motor Vehicle Act* and the *Criminal Code*. Under the MVA she could pay a $100 fine for a first offence.

Under the *Criminal Code*, though, it is much more serious. She can face up to five years' imprisonment for doing any of the following when involved in an accident:

- failing to stop;
- failing to give her name and address; or
- failing to offer assistance at the accident scene.

To be convicted, she must have had a mental intent to "escape civil or criminal liability." This may be assumed by the court if she does not offer any good reasons for leaving.

Drinking and Driving Offences

DEAR LISA

   I had my driver's licence suspended for a year by the court for drinking and driving. I was caught last week driving while prohibited. The police have charged me with failing to obey a court order. What kind of trouble am I in?

WALKING SOBER

DEAR SOBER

   You may be in quite a bit of trouble. If your case is being heard in the Halifax courts, you may face an automatic 30-day jail sentence for breaching a court order, depending on which judge hears your case. I strongly suggest you have legal representation before making your plea and/or being sentenced.

DEAR LISA

   I was caught drinking and driving last Saturday night. I wasn't in an accident and it's my first offence. What will my sentence be if I plead guilty?

FEELING IRRESPONSIBLE

DEAR IRRESPONSIBLE

   The sentence varies somewhat depending on where in the province you are sentenced. The *Criminal Code* requires a minimum fine of $500 and a 1-year suspension of your driver's licence. If you are sentenced in Halifax, the courts often impose an $800 to a $1,000 fine for a first-time offence.

DEAR LISA

   Last month, the police charged me with "care and control of a motor vehicle" while drinking. I had returned home and parked my car in my building's parkade. I left my car running because my dog was in it. It was hot and she needed the air conditioning. I had a couple of beers with my buddy for the 20 minutes I had my car running. I was about 15 metres away from my car when the police drove up to me. How can they charge me with this offence if I was not intending to use my car again?

GOOD INTENTIONED

DEAR GOOD INTENTIONED

The *Criminal Code* offence of care and control of a vehicle while impaired has been interpreted very strictly by judges, and not in your favour. For instance, cases have consistently resulted in convictions of drivers who sleep off their drunkenness in their cars, even when the car is not running.

Some of the court's considerations are:

- the accessibility of the keys to the person charged, and
- whether the person charged has the immediate means of putting the vehicle in motion (regardless of the person's intention).

For example, if you sleep off your drunkenness while in your car and you throw the keys in the trunk, which now you cannot access, the Crown probably could not win a conviction. In your case, however, you may still end up being found guilty because you had your keys with you and you were relatively near your car (i.e., you were not in your house, in bed).

On the other hand, your facts are unique. A judge may consider your actions of drinking after you had driven and the dog requiring air conditioning enough facts to raise a reasonable doubt as to whether you had care and control. You may want to take this one to trial.

DEAR LISA

I was convicted of dangerous driving under the *Criminal Code*. My licence has been revoked by the Registry of Motor Vehicles for five years. How can they do that if the judge didn't order a suspension as part of my sentence?

ROAD RAGE

DEAR ROAD RAGE

A suspension of your licence for a dangerous-driving conviction is not mandatory under the *Criminal Code*.

The *Motor Vehicle Act*, though, also has jurisdiction and the Registrar of Motor Vehicles must impose a suspension for certain criminal code offences. In your case, a dangerous-driving conviction has a mandatory 5-year suspension under section 67 of the *Motor Vehicle Act*, apart from the *Criminal Code* punishment.

DEAR LISA

I have been caught drinking and driving for the second time. What will my punishment be for a second offence?

SLOWLY LEARNING

DEAR LEARNING

Fourteen days in jail is the mandatory sentence for a second conviction if you are served with the Crown's notice of intention to increase your penalty. You also lose your driver's licence for three years. For three or more convictions, there is a mandatory 90 days in jail and you lose your licence for a minimum of 10 years.

DEAR LISA

The police stopped my friend the other day for drinking and driving. He blew more than .05 but was less than .08 for alcohol in the blood. They took his car away for 24 hours. Does he get a criminal record too?

WALKING THE STRAIGHT LINE

DEAR WALKING

No, he does not get a criminal record. The *Motor Vehicle Act* gives a 24-hour suspension of your driver's licence if you blow higher then .05 but less than .08 for blood alcohol. Breathing between .05 and .08 is not a *Criminal Code* offence and, therefore, your friend will not get a criminal record. The police probably towed his car because there was no one available to drive it home. If your friend has a graduated (beginner's) license, he will have to serve an additional two years in the Graduated Licensing Program.

DEAR LISA

For drinking and driving offences, can the police get a blood sample instead of using the Breathalyzer? My friend knew someone who had been convicted of drunk driving because the police took a blood sample. If it is true, how does that work?

HOLDING MY BREATH

DEAR HOLDING

If the police have reasonable and probable grounds to believe that a person is "incapable" of giving a breath sample or it is "impracticable," they can demand a blood sample (s. 254(3)(b) *Criminal Code*). The police do not actually take the blood sample but request a doctor take the sample. The doctor must first confirm that it would not endanger the life or health of the suspect.

A person can refuse to give a blood (or breath) sample, in which case the police would charge them with failing to provide a sample. This charge has a similar punishment to breathing over the limit.

If a person is unconscious, the police can also get a warrant to collect the blood sample. The police, themselves, are not allowed to collect blood even if it is readily available, for example, from blood flowing freely from a person's wound at the scene of an accident (*R. v. Tomaso*, Ont. C.A.). The courts have deemed this to be a violation of a person's right to privacy and a person's right not to self-incriminate.

Young Offenders

DEAR LISA

I was just arrested for joy riding with my friends in a stolen car. I have no criminal record. Will I go to jail? I am only 14 years old and really scared.

HIGH-PRICED JOY

DEAR HIGH-PRICED JOY

No. You should ask the Crown attorney if you can go through youth diversion called Restorative Justice. This program, if you take responsibility for the offence, will allow you to be diverted out of the criminal courts and into a mediation-type setting. You typically meet with the victim and a plan is worked out for compensation and an apology. If you successfully complete the program, you do not get a criminal record. If you are charged with something again, however, you may go to criminal court.

DEAR LISA

I'm 16 years old and I have just been charged with prostitution. I have no previous criminal record. If I am convicted, will I go to jail?

ON THE STREETS

DEAR STREETS

No. If found guilty, you would probably get a fine ($100 to $300) and/or probation. You may be able, though, to avoid criminal court altogether. If you are willing to accept responsibility for the offence, ask the Crown attorney prosecuting your case if you can go to School 213, which is a type of diversion program, instead of court. For further assistance, you can also call Coverdale (902-422-6417), an organization that helps accused women in the criminal courts.

There is also a self-help group called Go Girls, run by women who have formerly worked in the trade. This group offers education and support through weekly meetings. You can contact Go Girls at Coverdale as well.

DEAR LISA

Can a department store sue me because my son was caught shoplifting there? They just sent me a letter threatening to sue me.

TROUBLED PARENT

DEAR TROUBLED PARENT

There is more smoke than fire in that letter. Large department stores are beginning to send out letters threatening to sue the parents of children who have shoplifted. In this case, the store has to prove that you were responsible for the actions of your child at the time of the theft, which would be extremely difficult. Sometimes kids do irresponsible things due to no fault of their parents.

The store could take legal action against your child (assuming they did not recover the stolen goods). But because the pockets of children tend to be very shallow, the store is attempting to come after you, the parent, instead. The department store probably does not have the legal right to sue you. Even if they could convince a judge to hear it, the legal fees would be likely too expensive to be worth their while.

ৎ৩৯ ৎ৩৯ ৎ৩৯

DEAR LISA

My 16-year old son was recently approached by two police officers and arrested as he was walking home from school. He was asked to identify himself, which he did, and then told to proceed to the police station. Once at the station, he was told that he was the only suspect in a house break-in based on an anonymous tip and no other information. After the police questioned him, he was released without being charged.

I have a pretty good idea who would make such a malicious, false accusation against my son. I am angry at that person, but I am more angry at the police for arresting a 16-year old kid based on hearsay information. Can the police arrest someone based solely on an anonymous tip? Do we have grounds to sue the police for damages?

PEEVED PAPA

DEAR PEEVED

The police officers are allowed to arrest your son if they had "reasonable and probable grounds to believe he had committed an indictable offence" (s.495 of the *Criminal Code*). Break and enter into a private dwelling home is, in fact, an indictable offence that carries a maximum punishment of life imprisonment. Therefore, if they had reasonable and probable grounds to think your son was involved, they could arrest him.

An anonymous tip, however, is probably not considered reasonable and probable grounds. While the police are not required to confirm a witness's information as being true (*R. v. Golub*, Ont. C.A.), the witness should give detailed information and not claim anonymity. Because the call was anonymous, it would be difficult for the police to assess the informant's reliability. It seems your son would have been saved the trauma of arrest if the police had required greater reliability from their source.

Although the arrest was probably unlawful, the police officers were still "acting in the execution of their duties," which gives them a lot of protection against you suing them. You may ask the police, though, to consider a public mischief charge against the person who gave the tip.

Assault

DEAR LISA

I am charged with assaulting my wife by grabbing her arm to move her away from me. The Crown attorney told me they are not allowed to send me to adult diversion because it was a "domestic violence" charge. Otherwise, he said I would have been a good candidate. It doesn't seem fair. What can I do?

FEARING THE WORST

DEAR FEARING

The Attorney General's directive states that the Crown and police "shall not" redirect spousal violence matters through adult diversion. Adult diversion would have allowed you to avoid criminal court and a possible conviction. Politically, there was concern that spousal violence would be perceived as being taken lightly if all cases of domestic violence were not criminally prosecuted.

The case of *R. v. Boudreau* (NS) recently confirmed this lack of adult diversion for spousal violence is not contrary to the *Charter*.

DEAR LISA

The police just charged my neighbour with assaulting her child with a weapon. She apparently hit her with a belt to discipline her. I thought you could use corporal punishment on a child as long as you are the parent?

TIGHTENING MY OWN BELT

DEAR TIGHTENING

You are correct, but within limits. Section 43 of the *Criminal Code* provides that: "Every school teacher, parent, or person standing in the place of a parent is justified in using force by way of correction toward a pupil or child . . . who is under his [sic] care, if the force used does not exceed what is reasonable under the circumstances."

Some of the things judges consider in deciding what is reasonable are:

- the age of the child and the severity of the punishment (the younger the child, the less severe the punishment should be);

- the kind of behaviour being corrected (the more extreme or disruptive the child's behaviour, the more force can be used);

- whether any injury occurs to the child;

- a reasonable connection between the choice of punishment and curbing the behaviour of the child (it would not be proper to spank a 1-year-old to get the child to stop crying when the child would not even understand why it was happening).

Judges have interpreted section 43 in different ways. Rarely, if ever, for example, is it acceptable to cause bruising or injury to the child.

(My thanks to Kim Richardson at Richardson's Law Office for his research and comments).

Miscellaneous

DEAR LISA

A couple of weeks ago, I had a forest fire on my lot of land. I was burning brush on a Wednesday and extinguished the fire. It smouldered for two days and then ignited on Friday, when it was unusually hot. How much trouble am I in? The fire trucks had to come and everything.

ALL FIRED UP

DEAR ALL FIRED UP

The Department of Natural Resources tells me that most typical fines are levied for failing to properly extinguish a fire or failing to have a permit. Both offences carry a $215 fine. The municipality also has similar offences that have fines ranging from $100 to $5,000, with tickets typically in the $100 range. Warning tickets may be given, instead.

If the fire has to be extinguished, you can also be ordered to pay restitution (repayment) for the often huge costs of extinguishing the fire. This is not often done, but it is more likely if the damage was severe or if you were extremely negligent.

DEAR LISA

My 17-year-old son has a girlfriend who is only 15 years old. I think they have become sexually active. What is the legal age for sexual contact?

FATHERLY CONCERN

DEAR CONCERN

Fourteen years old is the legal age, as long as the older person is not in a position of trust, for example, a babysitter. The *Criminal Code* prohibits sexual contact with someone younger than 14 years old. Therefore, lack of knowledge of age cannot be used as a defence by an accused at trial.

There is, however, an exception. Persons between the ages of 12 to 14 years old can consent to sexual contact if the other person is younger than 16, and less than two years older than the complainant. Your son can have sexual contact with his girlfriend.

It's "Divorce Barbie."
It comes with only the clothes on her back.

Family

Adoption

DEAR LISA

My current husband would like to adopt my 5-year-old child. Do I need the biological father's consent? What if the father will not give the consent?

STEPPING INTO THE FUTURE

DEAR STEPPING

The *Children and Family Services Act* governs adoptions in the province. Your child's father must receive formal notice of the adoption hearing, be given relevant documents and consent to the adoption. A judge can dispense or do away with the biological father's consent if:

- the father has not had contact with the child for two years prior to the adoption placement, or

- the father has not paid child support for two years prior to the adoption placement, or

- the court feels given "all the circumstances of the case" the father's consent should be dispensed with if it is in the best interests of the adopted person.

While there are other considerations the judge can also take into account, a judge has full discretion to dispense with the father's consent as long as it is in your child's best interest.

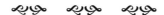

Marriage/Marriage Contracts

DEAR LISA

I am getting married but I don't belong to a church. Can I have my wedding at the courthouse and how much does it cost?

A CIVIL FIANCEE

DEAR FIANCEE

You can have the wedding at the courthouse for a cost of $50. You must bring the marriage licence for the judge to sign, which costs $100. Marriage licences are obtained from the Vital Statistics office of Service Nova Scotia and Municipal Relations (www.gov.ns.ca/snsmr/vstat), not the courthouse.

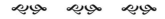

DEAR LISA

What is the difference between a cohabitation agreement and a prenuptial agreement?

SORTING IT OUT

DEAR SORTING IT OUT

A cohabitation agreement is a marriage contract for people who are not married but live together. A prenuptial agreement is a marriage contract made in preparation for marriage (prenuptial) and comes into effect when the couple wants it to, either right away or upon marriage. Both contracts can be worded so that they accomplish the same thing, for example, a cohabitation agreement can be worded to cover eventual marriage.

DEAR LISA

I inherited some property years before I met my husband-to-be. Do all properties deeded in my name also become his property when we marry?

PRE-WEDDING QUESTIONS

DEAR QUESTIONS

Inheritances are not normally divisible under the *Matrimonial Property Act*. The big exception, however, is if he has been directly involved with the property, he may be able to make a claim to some of it.

Assets that are used by the family during marriage – regardless of who buys them – are divided 50-50. If you do not like this division of property, I recommend a marriage contract which would stipulate who gets what if your marriage breaks down.

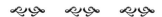

DEAR LISA

I got married last year. I owned my home prior to this marriage and it is paid for in full. Do I have to give my wife half of it if we split up? What can I do?

LOVE IN THE HEART, AIR IN THE BRAIN

DEAR LOVE IN THE HEART

I strongly recommend a marriage contract which can be drawn up now, even after you are married. This contract will define who gets what upon marriage breakdown. The contract can be worded to state the parties leave the marriage with what they brought into it. The longer your wife lives in the house with you, the greater the claim she can make to it, unless you have a contract that states otherwise.

It is preferable to decide these issues while you are getting along, rather than waiting until your relationship has broken down (if that happens). It also can be a wonderful way to get to know your partner!

DEAR LISA

Does my name change automatically when I get married this August?

BRIDE TO BE

DEAR BRIDE TO BE

No, your name does not automatically change. Historically the name change signified a change in possession of the woman from the father to the husband. This change in possession explains the tradition of your father "giving you away" at your wedding. Ouch! Unless you change it, your name will remain as it is.

Child Support

DEAR LISA

If I declare bankruptcy, will that eliminate my arrears in child support? A court has ordered me to pay $13,000 in back support.

FEELING THE PINCH

DEAR FEELING THE PINCH

No. You can eliminate most other debts, but not child support arrears.

DEAR LISA

My oldest daughter who is living with my ex will be attending university next year. My ex wants me to pay 50 percent of her university costs. Our annual incomes are the same; we both make $50,000 per year. If my daughter works during the summer and makes $4,000 and gets a $3,000 student loan, do we have to share the remaining costs?

PROUD PAPA

DEAR PROUD

University tuition costs are a special or extraordinary expense under the *Federal Child Support Guidelines* (s.7 (1)(e)). The parents' contributions toward tuition are often paid proportional to their incomes. In your case, you and your ex would normally split the costs since your incomes are the same.

The child's summer wages may also be deducted from the amount the parents have to contribute. Cases have consistently held that the child is obligated to contribute summer wages to reduce school costs. Judges have gone as far as imputing them to the child, should they fail to get summer employment (*Simpson v. Palma*, [1998] S.J. 581 (Q.B.)).

The cases are more divided on whether a child should be obligated to get a student loan before they can rely on their parents' help. It appears the more money the parents have, the less likely judges will factor in the availability of a student loan. In your case, your combined income of $100,000 is quite high and a judge may not require your child to go into debt as part of her contribution. You and your ex would probably share school expenses after your child has contributed earnings, but before taking a student loan.

DEAR LISA

Can I get an increase in child support from my ex-husband? I am returning to the paid work force and will have increased child care costs.

DOUBLE BURDENED

DEAR DOUBLE BURDENED

Most likely. Often, you can get more child support when you return to work and have to pay extra child care costs. Payments for this expense would be paid proportional to both of your incomes. For example, if your husband makes twice as much as you, he may pay twice as much of the extra child care costs. These costs are called "special expenses" under the *Federal Child Support Guidelines* (s.7 (1)(a) and (2)).

DEAR LISA

I am getting behind in my child maintenance and I am worried my wages are going to be garnished. How much would be taken off my paycheque if that happened?

HEDGING MY BETS

DEAR HEDGING

The Maintenance Enforcement Program will deduct 25 percent from your gross wages to pay any arrears. Your regular maintenance payment will then also be deducted from what pay is left. If your employer fails to make the required deductions, they can be held liable for these funds and could also be fined. Finally, there is an additional $75 administration fee, which will be deducted for every notice of garnishment issued.

DEAR LISA

I have a daughter who lives with my ex-wife. This child is 21 years old, not in school and working full time. When am I legally entitled to stop my child support payments?

LOOKING TO THE FUTURE

DEAR LOOKING

The courts have consistently said that parents can stop financially supporting an able bodied (and mentally competent) child when the earliest of one of the following events occurs:

- The child is 16 or older and working full time (i.e., she is supporting herself financially);
- If the child is in school, support continues until she is finished her first degree or diploma; or
- The child has reached the age of 24 years old.

You probably should not be paying child support; however, you need to apply to the court to have it terminated if your wife does not agree to the change.

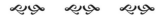

DEAR LISA

Can my ex-wife refuse to let me see my children because I can't afford my child support payments?

FLAT BROKE

DEAR FLAT BROKE

No, your ex-wife must let you see the children. The courts are very clear that access will never be affected even though you have not been able to pay your child support. The "best interests of the child" demand that the relationship between the father and the child continue whether or not maintenance has been paid.

If you cannot afford to pay because you have lost your job (or some other change in circumstance), you should immediately apply to the court to lower your payments. If you do not, you risk owing back-payments.

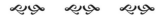

DEAR LISA

My husband wants to have a marriage contract that stipulates how much child support will be paid in the event we split up and I take the children. I am afraid if I sign an agreement now, I may regret it because I won't know the cost of raising our kids in the future. What should I do?

IN A CORNER

DEAR IN A CORNER

Not to worry. The child support part of the contract is not enforceable even if you sign it. The courts have the final say over the rights of your children. The courts will consider the income of the payor at the time of separation to determine the amount of child support. They are not bound by child support agreements in marriage contracts.

DEAR LISA

Who pays the taxes on child support payments, my ex-wife who has the children or me?

OVERTAXED

DEAR OVERTAXED

If your support payments were ordered after May 1, 1997, you do not get to deduct child support payments and your ex-wife does not have to claim it as income. If the order pre-dates May 1, 1997, and has not been changed by a court since then, your wife claims it as income, and you take a tax deduction. The entire family unit financially benefits having your wife claim it if she is in a lower tax bracket than you. So you may want to leave the old order as is, if you have one.

DEAR LISA

My 15-year-old son has moved out of our home against our wishes. He is staying with his best friend and the friend's mother. My son contacted social services for benefits, but they told him that we have to pay child support to the person he is staying with. Do I have to pay? The support I offer is a home and a bed to sleep in.

COUNTING THE YEARS TO ADULTHOOD

DEAR COUNTING

Hang in there. You may have to pay support to the person taking care of your child. This person or your child, though, would have to make an application to the family court for this support if you do not voluntarily pay it. Child support is usually paid until the child is working full-time or has finished their first degree or trade diploma.

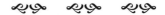

Spousal Support

DEAR LISA

I think I am the only person in Canada who does not have a cut-off date for their spousal support payments. My ex-wife and I were married for 18 years. We have three grown children and have been separated for the past 10 years. We are both 55 years old. She is functionally illiterate and makes about $15,000 per year. I am an architect and make about $80,000 per year. I currently pay $400 per month. Am I in this for the long haul?

ISOLATED

DEAR ISOLATED

It's looking like the long haul. The Supreme Court of Canada (*Moge v. Moge*) considered a similar fact situation where the wife had a very low level of education (grade 7) and the marriage was long-term (about 18 years). The court said that the duty for a spouse to become economically independent has limits. Factors like the length of the marriage and the realistic ability of the spouse to become independent are considered. The court also recognized that women were disproportionately impoverished by divorce (particularly due to their traditional role as homemaker) and awarding spousal support is a way to address this disadvantage.

A more recent Supreme Court of Canada decision (*Bracklow v. Bracklow*) further broadened/clarified the ability of a spouse to receive long-term spousal support. In this case, the Court found that the need for support did not have to be tied to an "economic disadvantage stemming from the marriage." It was enough that one spouse has the need and the other, the ability to pay.

Given these decisions, you may have to pay her support indefinitely.

Legal Costs

DEAR LISA

I am taking my wife to court to reduce the spousal support I pay her. My lawyer thinks we will win. If so, can I get legal costs from her? Is it common for the family courts to award them?

WINNING WAYS

DEAR WINNING

If you win your case in the family court, our Court of Appeal has said judges should award costs to you unless there is a "good reason not to" (*Kaye v. Campbell*). Nonetheless, costs are not commonly asked for by lawyers in the family division due to earlier court decisions that discouraged them.

If you do ask for them, however, judges are obligated to award costs to the winning party unless there are certain reasons such as:

- There was misconduct by the successful party before or during the trial (e.g., lying or making unfounded accusations);

- There was only partial success on the issues raised at trial;

- The assets and income of the losing party are such that costs against them would create a hardship.

Divorce/Procedure

DEAR LISA

I have to take my ex-husband to court to decrease his access and increase his child support. I'm pretty sure he's not going to consent. What is the court process and how long will it take for this to get to trial?

MAKING SOME CHANGES

DEAR CHANGES

If you live in Halifax and unless it's an emergency, your ex-husband can relax for the next year. The Supreme Court (Family Division) has just had some judicial appointments, but there is still a backlog. By comparison, if you live in Windsor, you can likely get a trial within six weeks.

In Halifax, there are quite a few stops along the way before you get to a hearing:

1. If you do not have a lawyer, you will need to make an intake appointment with the family court intake worker.

2. The intake worker assigns you a conciliation date with your ex-husband to see if it is possible to resolve the case through a family court worker.

3. If conciliation fails, you will be given a docket appearance notice, which will be your first appearance in front of a judge. If you have a lawyer, your lawyer normally skips to step three.

4. At the docket appearance, you will be given an organizational pre-trial date with a judge. At this time, the judge discusses how many witnesses there will be at the hearing and what type of evidence will be called. This judge is normally your trial judge.

5. At the organizational pre-trial, you will be given a settlement-oriented pre-trial date. The settlement pre-trial is your second formal opportunity to achieve a settlement. You have a good chance of settling at this stage.

6. If there is no settlement achieved at the settlement pre-trial, you are given a trial date.

7. At your trial, you will have a court order deciding the issues one way or another.

DEAR LISA

My mother has been divorced twice. Is it possible to get these two marriages annulled on the grounds of physical and mental abuse?

PROTECTIVE DAUGHTER

DEAR PROTECTIVE DAUGHTER

No. You cannot get a legal annulment (which is different than a religious annulment) for these reasons. Physical and mental abuse are grounds for a divorce, not an annulment. A marriage can only be legally annulled if there was a defect in the validity of the marriage. For example, if a person is mentally incompetent, a marriage can be annulled. Marrying someone under duress (a shotgun wedding) would be another example of grounds for an annulment. When an annulment is granted by a court, it is as if the marriage never happened. The parties would return to their pre-married financial state, too. The *Matrimonial Property Act*, for example, would not apply.

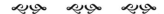

DEAR LISA
Can I refuse to give my husband a divorce?

HURTIN' HEART

DEAR HURTIN'
No. You have to let him go. He can divorce you after separating from you for one year.

DEAR LISA
How much does an uncontested divorce cost? We already have a separation agreement.

FREE AT LAST

DEAR FREE AT LAST
Lawyers' fees vary; however, the usual court filing fees and related expenses are about $300. There are as many as 12 legal documents that have to be prepared to get the divorce.

You can also do the divorce yourself. The family court sells the forms on computer disks for $10. Many of my clients, however, have found them confusing. I also caution that if you do it yourself, you should have a lawyer review your separation agreement and the final draft of your divorce documents. She can ensure that your divorce documents actually reflect what is in your separation agreement. Many important legal rights which you need to protect are defined upon divorce.

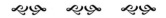

DEAR LISA

How long do I have to wait for my divorce if we agree on everything?

SEPARATED

DEAR SEPARATED

If your grounds for divorce are that you have been living "one year separate and apart," you can get a divorce one year from your separation date.

If one of you committed adultery or cruelty to the other, you could get your divorce much earlier. This person must voluntarily sign an affidavit admitting to the adultery or cruelty. If so, you can get a divorce immediately (although it can still take two to six months in Halifax for the court to process the divorce papers).

If they will not sign an affidavit admitting to the adultery or cruelty, you would have to have a trial to establish these grounds. A trial would take more than a year to be heard which is why most people get a divorce using the ground "one year separate and apart."

Separation Agreements

DEAR LISA

My wife and I don't talk any more and I want to get a divorce. My kids deserve a happier family life. Where do I start?

WORN OUT

DEAR WORN OUT

The first step is normally a formal separation agreement, which is a contract between the parties. It confirms and binds the parties' agreement on custody, access, maintenance (child and spousal), and property division.

If you get these matters negotiated, you can then apply for an uncontested divorce. When you have a separation agreement, the divorce is merely paperwork and you do not need to show up at court.

If you cannot negotiate these issues, you have a divorce hearing and a judge decides them instead. This process can be very costly. A contested divorce can cost from $5,000 to $20,000 depending on the complexity, and it can take years to get.

DEAR LISA

I recently discovered my ex-husband had squirreled away about $100,000 worth of RRSPs during our 20-year marriage. He failed to disclose this information to me when we were negotiating our divorce. In the divorce, we each got half of the house, which was all I thought we had. What can I do?

EVEN HAPPIER TO BE DIVORCED

DEAR EVEN HAPPIER

A standard separation agreement (which is the foundation document defining the terms of a divorce) has a clause that states both parties have given full financial disclosure to the other. Since your ex-husband apparently "overlooked" this asset, the court will allow you to vary your divorce order and probably give you half of the RRSPs. The court may also order him to pay you solicitor-client legal costs (which are more than regular "party-party" costs) and/or award punitive (punishing) damages for his omission.

Child Custody/Access

DEAR LISA

What is sole custody? How is it different than joint custody? My lawyer recommends that I agree to share joint custody with my ex-husband. I don't want to lose any of my rights. What should I do?

BETWIXT AND BETWEEN

DEAR BETWIXT

There is a legal presumption that both parents are entitled to joint custody of the child upon separation. If the parents, however, have so much conflict between them that they could not decide the major decisions in the child's life together (such as schooling, religion, and health care), then one of the parents will be awarded sole custody.

Unless there is a high level of conflict between the two of you, I recommend joint custody. People are often concerned about the labels "sole or joint" when what really affects your life is how much actual time you get with the child. It is often better to focus your time and money negotiating these important details rather than the label of joint or sole custody.

DEAR LISA

What grounds must Community Services have to take away my two children?

CONCERNED PARENT

DEAR PARENT

A social worker must have "reasonable and probable grounds to believe a child is in need of protective services and the child's health or safety cannot be protected adequately otherwise than by taking the child into care" (s.33, *Children and Family Services Act*).

Within five days of taking the children, Community Services must have the matter brought before a judge. Community Services must then show that there are "reasonable and probable grounds to believe the child is in need of protective services" (s.39(3)).

If Community Services still has the children under their care after this time, there are various mandatory reviews by a judge that must occur. Eventually they may have the right to take your children permanently if they can show they "are in need of protective services" living under your care (s. 40).

DEAR LISA

The father of my two boys sexually molested them and went to jail for a year. We don't have an agreement yet on access. When he gets out, can I refuse to give him access?

APPREHENSIVE

DEAR APPREHENSIVE

Often, supervised access is granted by a court, even under these circumstances. The courts, though, look at a lot of circumstances to determine the best interests of the children. Severe abuse and other bad circumstances, such as drug use, make it possible to have a total denial of access, although it is rare. You may want to consider having your children see a psychologist, who could assist you and the court on whether there should be any access.

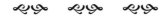

Custody and Moving Out of Province

DEAR LISA

I want to have joint custody of my children so my wife can't leave the province without my input. She has day-to-day care and control of them. Is this a good solution?

A HANDS-ON DAD

DEAR HANDS-ON

Joint custody will not necessarily take care of this problem. Joint custody does give you input into the major decisions of your children's lives. If you think, however, she may move out of the province, the issue of whether she can, and on what terms, should be specifically written into the custody agreement.

If you merely ask for joint custody, and your agreement is silent on this mobility issue, she could leave the province without consulting you. You would then be in the position of having to make an emergency application to prevent her from leaving, or, if she had left, ordering the children returned to the province.

Custody agreements often stipulate that:

- The custodial parent will give the access parent advance notice of an intended move, or
- The custodial parent must have written permission of the other

parent or have a court order before they permanently leave the province.

DEAR LISA

I have just broken up with the father of my child. Although we have always lived in Nova Scotia, I want to go to Ontario to look for work and take our four-year-old with me. The father lives here in Nova Scotia. Can I leave the province without his consent? Is it kidnapping if I do?

LOOKING FOR A NEW LIFE

DEAR LOOKING

You may be kidnapping and/or abducting your child if you leave without his consent.

Do you have either a written agreement or court order that gives you custody and states that you have "primary care and control" over the children? Even if you do have this agreement or custody order, and there is nothing in the order that prevents you from leaving Nova Scotia, you can still be charged with abduction. You should give the father at least one month's written notice, your new address and phone number. If you do not, the court may consider that you are trying to block his access. If the family court were left with this impression, they may not allow your child to leave the province and/or the police could charge you if you block his access.

Matrimonial Property

DEAR LISA

Can I get more in the divorce settlement, if my wife had a one-night stand at the local hotel?

BETRAYED

DEAR BETRAYED

No. The *Matrimonial Property Act* governs how property is divided. Fault causing the marriage breakdown is not given consideration when determining how property will be divided. Under the Act, the wife and husband are each presumed to have a 50 percent interest in the "matrimonial property." Business assets and inheritances are generally not divisible, but there are exceptions.

DEAR LISA

I have a life insurance policy that lists my children as the beneficiaries. Would my children still be entitled to the insurance benefits upon my death if I live common law with my current boyfriend or if I get married?

LOOKING OUT FOR MY KIDS

DEAR LOOKING OUT

Yes. Your children would still be entitled to your life insurance benefits as long as they are listed as the beneficiaries on the policy. The *Matrimonial Property Act* and the common law do not interfere with these designations. Your partner will have no claim to these funds.

DEAR LISA

If I have a joint bank account with my child from another marriage, would my current husband be entitled to any money in the account in the event of marriage breakdown?

GETTING SMART

DEAR GETTING SMART

This is certainly a good way to muddy the waters when dividing up assets. Your spouse would have an argument for some of the money if he could show that the money was really yours and that it was earned during the years you were married to him. If your child is the only one that contributes to the account (and you only have your name on the account as a formality), then your spouse would not be entitled to the money.

DEAR LISA

I understand I am entitled to 50 percent of the matrimonial assets if we separate. Is it possible to get more than this?

EXPLORING ALL MY OPTIONS

DEAR EXPLORING

A recent case in Ontario allowed the wife to take more than half of the assets. In this case, the judge agreed the husband had incurred a lot of the debt because of strip-club and phone-sex activities for two years before the breakup. Alcoholism or excessive gambling are other circumstances in which judges have ordered an unequal division. Also, an unequal split can be ordered when one person has made a larger down payment on a home in a short-term marriage (one to three years, for example).

DEAR LISA

I am a single parent and I had a common-law relationship for five years. Unfortunately, we broke up about two years ago. I got interim exclusive possession of the home. Is there a law anywhere that says if a person vacates the home for a period of time, he is no longer considered eligible to be on the deed?

EX-BURDENED

DEAR EX-BURDENED

No, in this situation you cannot gain more ownership rights to the house simply by having possession of it for an extended period of time. A court order, consent or death are the only ways to get him off the deed.

If he dies, for example, his interest will go to you if you two are listed as "joint tenants" on the deed. (Vice versa, if you die.) If you were listed as tenants in common, though, his interest would go to his estate.

DEAR LISA

Since we broke up, my ex's lawyers have put two $5,000 judgments on our home. He incurred the debt to the lawyers since our breakup. Our home is up for re-mortgage next month and he still says he will not sign the home over to me. Is there any way I can get him off the deed now?

DOUBLE EX-BURDENED

DEAR DOUBLE EX

It sounds like you need to make an application to the court to have the house ordered into your name or to sell it. If you are awarded the house, you would still have to buy out his interest in it (however much that may be) unless you can offset it with something he owes you. The judgments on the house are his responsibility alone, and he would have to pay them from his share.

Pensions

DEAR LISA

All I hear about is how my wife's divorced friends are going to get half of their husbands' pensions when they retire from work. I was severely wounded in Vietnam and get a disability pension for injuries I received. Is my wife entitled to half of these monies if she goes her own way? She was not in my life at that time.

JUST WONDERING

DEAR JUST WONDERING

She would not be entitled to a division of the pension as an asset since you earned it prior to being married to her and it is currently in stream to you.

If she has an entitlement to spousal support, however, a judge would consider your pension income. Both parties' incomes regardless of their sources are considered although there are many other factors relevant in determining her eligibility (or yours) to support.

DEAR LISA

My wife and I are separating. My wife has worked for the school board for 20 years and I understand I am entitled to half of her pension.

She has another five years until her retirement. Can my share of her pension be rolled over into an RRSP, like federal pensions?

PREPARING THE RETIREMENT NEST

DEAR PREPARING

No, the Nova Scotia *Pension Benefits Act* does not allow an immediate rollover into a retirement savings vehicle. You are entitled, though, to a separate pension account that will pay you the pension directly when your wife retires or on her normal retirement date, whichever is earlier.

When this account has been set up by the pension administrator at the school board, your portion of her pension will not be affected by the death of your wife. Similarly, if you die after this account has been set up, your estate is entitled "to a refund of contributions plus interest" that your wife earned on your behalf for the duration of your marriage (s.61(4)(c)).

Matrimonial Debt

DEAR LISA

Am I liable for the debts of my husband? He is always taking out a loan to buy a new toy or gadget. I am the financially responsible one, and I don't want to get stuck with all this debt if we ever separate.

A FRUSTRATED THRIFT

DEAR FRUSTRATED THRIFT

Technically, no, you are only responsible for the debts of your husband if you co-sign or guarantee the debts. If you do not sign these debt contracts, they are strictly between your husband and the creditors.

When couples separate, however, the total debts created during the marriage are normally deducted from the total matrimonial assets. Only then are the assets usually divided between the parties. So, in effect, you could end up paying for half his debts even though you did not sign the original debt contract.

If you want to protect yourself from his spending habits, I strongly recommend you have a marriage contract signed between the two of you.

This agreement would stipulate that his debts are his alone in the event of separation.

DEAR LISA

If I default on my student loan payment after I get married, can the bank try to collect my loan payments from my wife?

FOR BETTER OR FOR WORSE

DEAR FOR BETTER OR FOR WORSE

No. Debts that you contract for in your name alone are not transferable to anyone else unless they actually sign (co-sign or guarantee) it. Marriage does not affect the debt contracts you have with third parties and does not make her liable for them.

If you separate, you may end up sharing matrimonial debt, even if your wife incurred the debt herself (but the debt should be related to marriage expenses). These debt obligations, though, are only between the two of you. For example, if you separate from your wife and she has a Visa bill for $1,000 in her name alone, Visa can only come after her for payment. If the Visa expenses are deemed matrimonial expenses (e.g., household expenses), then you may end up paying for $500 of it in the separation agreement. Only your wife, though, can come after you for this money, not Visa.

Common-Law Couples

DEAR LISA

I have been in a relationship for two years. I recently heard that the *Matrimonial Property Act* now applies to all common-law couples and not just married couples. Is this true that I automatically have to share all of my property 50-50?

FEELING IMPOSED UPON

DEAR FEELING IMPOSED UPON

No, this is not exactly accurate. This law has recently undergone great change. The Nova Scotia Court of Appeal decision of *Walsh v. Bona* recently decided that sections of the *Matrimonial Property Act* were unconstitutional because they did not apply equally to married and unmarried couples. The Court, however, suspended the effect of this declaration for 12 months to allow our legislature to change the Act to include common-law couples.

The legislature, in response, enacted a bill that came into force June 4, 2001. This bill allows common-law couples to be included under the *Matrimonial Property Act* if they register a "Domestic Partnership Declara-tion" with Vital Statistics (www.gov.ns.ca/snsmr/vstat).

Although your common-law relationship is not directly covered by the Act, if you and your partner register with Vital Statistics, you will be. On the other hand, if you do not sign the declaration, the Act does not apply to your property.

DEAR LISA

My same-sex partner and I want the same rights as straight couples? What are my civil rights?

CIVILLY RIGHT

DEAR CIVILLY

Your question is timely. Recent changes in the law created Domestic Partnership Declarations which not only give matrimonial property rights to common-law straight couples, but also to same-sex couples. Here are some of the other benefits available to you and common-law straight couples:

- The *Pension Benefits Act* – allows you or your partner to claim some portion of the other's pension upon relationship breakdown;

- The *Maintenance and Custody Act* (formerly the *Family Mainte-nance Act*) – allows spousal and child support to be paid;

- The *Matrimonial Property Act* – allows property to be divided upon breakdown of the relationship;

- The *Intestate Succession Act* – allows a partner to receive a portion of the deceased partner's estate in the event they do not have a will;
- The *Income Tax Act* (provincial) – stipulates what tax benefits are allowed for spouses (and is now consistent with the federal act).

To receive any of these rights, however, you must sign a Domestic Partnership Declaration (Vital Statistics: www.gov.ns.ca/snsmr/vstat).

DEAR LISA

My friend and her ex-boyfriend lived in a common-law relationship for three years. Shortly after moving in together, they got a dog. They broke up about six months ago and have been sharing the dog since then. Now, he has a new girlfriend who won't let my friend see the dog. What can she do? How do doggie custody battles work?

DOG FIGHT

DEAR DOG FIGHT

The courts will normally consider this doggie to be "chattel" or property. Therefore, access is not a typical remedy given by the court. Your friend may have to argue that she owns the dog and therefore she should have permanent possession of it. A judge in this case would consider who actually bought the dog and, possibly, who is primarily bonded with the dog.

If both are equally emotionally attached to the dog, a custody/access schedule is best negotiated between the parties. If not, they risk an all-or-nothing solution from a judge, treating it like property and giving it to one of the two parties, with no access to the other.

DEAR LISA

My partner and I have been living together for one year. Are we considered common law now? I understand there was new legislation this year on common-law couples.

COMMON BUT NOT PLAIN

DEAR COMMON

Your status as "common law" is often defined by legislation, depending on which law is governing your activity. For example, if you are seeking maintenance under the *Maintenance and Custody Act*, you must live in a conjugal (sexual) relationship for two years. The *Pensions Benefits Act* similarly defines common law as two years. On the other hand, the *Insurance Act* and the *Fatal Injuries Act* define common law as one year.

Just to add a little more confusion: If you both sign a Domestic Partnership Declaration (which you can register with Vital Statistics) and you are either living together or intending to live together, you do not have to wait the one or two years. When you sign the declaration, you immediately become defined as a common-law spouse. You can then take the benefits offered under the legislation discussed above and many other provincial acts.

The Tenacies Act says **written** *notice!*

Tenants/Landlords and -Ladies

Notice to Quit

DEAR LISA

Can I get out of my year-to-year lease with my landlady because I've become disabled and lost my job?

PERMANENTLY TERMINATED

DEAR PERMANENTLY

Yes. The *Residential Tenancies Act* (s.10C) allows you to give one month notice to your landlady. You, however, must provide her with a Medical

Certificate Form which you get from the Residential Tenacies Office at Service Nova Scotia and Municipal Relations.

ৼৢ৹ ৼৢ৹ ৼৢ৹

DEAR LISA

How much notice do I have to give my landlady if the lease is re-newed automatically every year?

MOVING ON

DEAR MOVING ON

Three months before the year is up on your lease (s.10 (1), *Residential Tenancies Act*).

ৼৢ৹ ৼৢ৹ ৼৢ৹

DEAR LISA

Can I get out of my year-to-year lease early if the landlady did not give me a copy of the *Residential Tenancies Act*?

CURIOUS

DEAR CURIOUS

Yes. If your landlady failed to give you a copy of the *Residential Tenancies Act* within 10 days of signing the lease, the Act (s.7(3)) allows you to terminate the lease. You must vacate the premises, however, on a specified day within the following three months.

If your landlady finally remembers to give you with a copy of the Act, you have one month to tell her you want to terminate the lease (but you still must quit within the three months). If you do not give her notice to quit within the month, you are stuck with your lease term.

If your landlady did not give you a written lease then the same rules apply, and you may terminate your lease early.

ৼৢ৹ ৼৢ৹ ৼৢ৹

DEAR LISA

Do I have to give my landlord written notice that I am leaving my apartment?

LEAVING

DEAR LEAVING

Yes. Proper notice to quit is defined in the *Residential Tenancies Act* as written notice. It should also contain your signature, the day you are terminating the tenancy, and the place you are vacating.

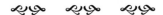

Eviction

DEAR LISA

I have a year-to-year lease and I am two months behind in the rent. How long does my landlady have to wait to evict me?

FALLING BEHIND

DEAR FALLING BEHIND

She can evict you at any moment. If you have a yearly or monthly tenancy, you have to be in arrears (any portion of the rent) for 30 days. She then has to give you 15 days' notice.

DEAR LISA

I just found out my tenants downstairs are part of a violent biker gang. I fear for my safety and the safety of my other tenants. How quickly can I evict them?

LANDLORD'S WORST NIGHTMARE

DEAR NIGHTMARE

If you think the biker tenants pose a risk to your safety or other tenants, you only have to give them a 5-day notice to quit (vacate) the premises.

DEAR LISA

I have a month-to-month lease with my landlady. She just told me I have one month to pack-up and leave, but I'm not in arrears and I have been an excellent tenant. Can she do that?

RELUCTANTLY PACKING

DEAR RELUCTANTLY PACKING

You can probably stop packing for a while. Your landlady must give you three months' notice to terminate your tenancy (s.10 *Residential Tenancies Act*), unless she can fit into one of the exceptions under the Act. You, on the other hand, only have to give her one month's notice.

You should also know:

- The eviction has to be in writing;
- The eviction should be personally served to you, or delivered by registered mail or courier;
- She does not have to give you a reason for asking you to leave.

DEAR LISA

Can my landlady seize my belongings to pay the rent after I have received an eviction notice?

EVICTED

DEAR EVICTED

Your landlady can seize your belongings only if she believes you have abandoned them. Even then, if she wants to sell them to pay for your arrears, she must receive permission from the Director of the Tenancy Board.

Damage Deposit

DEAR LISA

My landlord said he will deduct from my security deposit the cost of cleaning the carpet if I don't have it cleaned myself. I have been a very neat and clean tenant. Can he do that?

DOORMAT NO MORE

DEAR DOORMAT NO MORE

Unless your lease specifically requires you to clean the carpet when you vacate, your landlord is not allowed to charge you for "ordinary wear and tear" on the apartment, which includes carpet (and doormat) wear. For him to deduct any money from your security deposit, he must have a written consent form from the Residential Tenancies Office (www.gov.ns.ca/consumer/resten). If he deducts any money without your consent or without this permission form, you can file a complaint with the tenancies office.

Another tip when vacating is to take pictures of the apartment with fridge and stove doors open so you have proof that the place was clean.

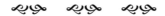

DEAR LISA

My landlady has asked for one month's security deposit because it is an expensive apartment that I am renting. I thought it was only allowed to be half of a month's rent. Is there a limit a landlady can ask for a security deposit?

CONFUSED

DEAR CONFUSED

You are correct. Under the *Residential Tenancies Act* (s.12(2)), your landlady can only ask for one half of a month's rent for a security deposit. You should also write out the physical conditions of the premises together with the landlady before you move in, so there is no dispute later about what was already damaged.

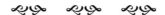

DEAR LISA

I had a fire in my apartment a couple months ago. My roommate left fat on the stove and the kitchen went up in flames. The landlord contacted me the other day and told me they are going to sue me for the $2,500 insurance deductable he had to pay. I wasn't even there when the fire happened, but we were both on the lease. Do we both have to pay?

ALL FIRED UP

DEAR ALL FIRED

The landlord can sue you but probably not successfully. He must show on a balance of probabilities that you, personally, were responsible for the fire. It sounds like it was your roommate, not you, who was negligent.

If you are served with Small Claims Court papers, however, be sure you file a defence and show up for the hearing. Otherwise, they can get a judgment against you.

Owner v. Tenant Liability for Injuries

DEAR LISA

I don't have a railing on the back deck of my home which is rented by tenants. If someone should be injured, who is responsible, me or the tenants?

LIABILITY CONSCIENCE

DEAR LIABILITY CONSCIENCE

Most likely, you will be held responsible. The test of liability under the *Occupier's Liability Act* asks: are the premises "reasonably safe"? You – as opposed to your tenant – are probably liable for any injuries at the home as a result of structural safety problems. The task of providing a railing on the deck would normally fall on you, and not your tenant, unless your lease stated otherwise. Your house insurance should cover any accidents on the premises.

Gee Toto, do you think our house insurance will cover this?

Personal Injury

Court Procedure

DEAR LISA

What are discoveries? My neighbour was injured in an accident and sued the other driver. Apparently she has discoveries next week.

NEIGHBOURLY INTEREST

DEAR NEIGHBOURLY INTEREST

Discoveries are pre-trial sworn testimony. Your neighbour will be asked, among other things, many questions about the accident itself, her work, educational and health background and her current state of health. A court reporter is hired who tape-records the testimony which is given at one of the two lawyers' offices.

The purpose of discoveries is to eliminate any surprises at trial. Both lawyers want to know all the facts before they go to court so they know the strengths and weaknesses of their case. The better each side understands the other's position, the greater the chance of negotiating a settlement.

DEAR LISA

My child has been injured in a car accident and we have to take the case to trial. How am I involved as the parent?

GETTING PREPARED

DEAR GETTING PREPARED

You or the child's other parent normally act as the "litigation guardian" or the Latin term is also used: *guardian ad litem*. You act for the child's best interests as a trustee. The lawyer would take instructions from you directly instead of the child.

DEAR LISA

I was badly injured in an accident and I have to testify at the trial. What tips can you give me for being a witness?

GETTING NERVOUS

DEAR GETTING NERVOUS

Here are a few tips for being a witness at a trial:

- Speak so the back of the courtroom can hear you. The microphones often do not amplify sound and only record the proceedings.

- When asked a question, generally address your answer to the judge, whom you refer to as "Your Honour" in Provincial Court and "My Lady" or "My Lord" in the Supreme Court.

- Although this may go without saying, tell the truth.

- If you cannot hear or you do not understand the question, ask the lawyer to repeat or to clarify it.

- Court is like church. Hats off, upscale your dress, and no gum chewing or candy. You want to show respect for the process.

- Finally, when being cross-examined, avoid being defensive or argumentative. No matter how aggressive the lawyer, try to treat her or him like a friendly acquaintance. This can be very difficult but it is often vital to your credibility.

DEAR LISA

I just found out that my father is dying of lung cancer. He has tried to quit smoking over the years more times than I can remember. Can I sue the cigarette company who sold him the cigarettes?

AN ANGRY DAUGHTER

DEAR ANGRY

Your father, more properly, would be the one to sue. In the United States, plaintiffs have had some recent success in pursuing these claims. We have not yet had any litigation in Canada that has set a precedent holding tobacco companies responsible for their dangerous products.

Also, in Nova Scotia, we do not have any class-action legislation that would allow a suit to be launched on behalf of all smokers similarly situated (although the Nova Scotia Barristers' Society is currently proposing this legislation). The claim currently would be restricted to your father's losses.

You may have difficulty finding a lawyer to represent you on contingency (taking a percentage of the award for the legal fee) because you may not win. Nova Scotia tends to be more conservative and therefore less inclined to make new law. If you were independently wealthy, though, you could pay a lawyer on an hourly rate to take it to trial.

Slip and Fall

DEAR LISA

I slipped on a grape in the grocery store produce section. I severely injured my back trying to catch myself in the fall. The grocery store tells me they will only pay for my physiotherapy. Can I sue for full compensation?

SUPER SORE

DEAR SUPER SORE

Your question is timely. Previously the answer was: If the store regularly checked the floors, you probably can not get any compensation. Recently, however, the Supreme Court of Nova Scotia (*Marche v. Empire Co. Ltd et al*) decided that grocery stores should also place rubber mats in produce areas, since there is such a high risk of food spilling. Therefore, if the store had no rubber mats in the produce section, you may have a good claim.

DEAR LISA

I was getting gas the other day when I slipped and fell on ice in the parking lot. There was a big patch of ice right in front of the door as I was going in to pay for the gas. I've missed a week of work. Can I sue?

DOWN BUT NOT OUT

DEAR DOWN

Yes, you can sue. If reasonable care was not taken to salt, sand and plow the parking lot, you will probably have a successful claim. Normally, businesses carry this kind of liability insurance. These claims can often be negotiated by your lawyer without having to sue.

DEAR LISA

I work as a cook in a restaurant. Last week, I slipped and fell on a puddle of water in the middle of the kitchen. Water had been leaking out of a pipe in the ceiling. I and other workers had complained about the problem, but they only fixed it after I fell. I am now off of work for six weeks. Can I sue?

NINE TO FIVE NO MORE

DEAR NINE TO FIVE

No, not if your employer pays into Workers' Compensation. The *Workers' Compensation Act* has virtually complete jurisdiction over most workplace accidents. Although it sounds like your employer was negligent in failing to fix the pipe leak earlier, Workers' Compensation will still cover claims even if they were caused by negligence. Also, there is paperwork for your employer to complete on the accident so you can make a claim to Workers' Compensation.

If you are self-employed or your boss does not pay into Workers' Compensation (the work sector is not covered by the Act), then you could sue your employer or the owner of the building directly. You would have to prove their negligence, though, which in your case appears fairly straightforward.

❧ ❧ ❧

Car Accident Injuries

DEAR LISA

Can I sue our own car insurance? I've been hurt in an accident, but my husband was driving and entirely at fault.

WONDERING WIFE

DEAR WONDERING

Yes. As a passenger, you can make a claim against your car insurance and receive compensation for your injury. If your insurance company is already paying for repairs to your car, your rates normally will not go up when they pay for your injury too. It is the number of accidents that increases your premiums, not normally the cost.

You should also:

- make this claim within two years of the date of the car accident;

- be aware that your husband, as the at-fault driver, would not be entitled to compensation, although he may want to spend some of yours.

DEAR LISA

I was just in an accident with my new car and I am missing time from work. Can I immediately get money from my car insurance to cover my wage losses?

MISSING TIME

DEAR MISSING TIME

Yes. Assuming you do not have any other coverage, you can get money from your own car insurance, but you have to be off work for at least six days. Your own car insurance company will pay you either $140 per week or 80 percent of your gross wage, whichever is less. These expenses are paid under section B of your policy, not by the person that hit you. They are no fault benefits, meaning they are paid out no matter who is at fault.

You should also know:

- a claim under section B should not increase your premium rates;
- these benefits are only available after you have used up any other insurance (e.g., disability insurance through work, EI coverage, etc.), or as a "top up" to these work benefits;
- your family doctor must confirm you are not able to work as a result of your accident injuries.

You can also get all medical costs paid for immediately. For example, keep your receipts for physiotherapy, massage therapy, mileage to medical appointments, chiropractic care, neck braces, crutches, etc. You may even be able to get a maid if you are a full-time homemaker and you cannot do your housework. Also, ask your insurance company if they will pay for the costs up-front instead of reimbursing you. Section B will cover these medical expenses even after you have settled your injury claim. The contract covers up to four years as long as the treatment is approved by your family doctor.

DEAR LISA

I was in a car accident with a friend who was driving. He had borrowed his boss's vehicle for the weekend to go fishing. There were serious injuries to the driver of the other vehicle and I have a knee injury. My friend's insurance company is refusing to provide any compensation. Can they do this?

KNEECAPPED

DEAR KNEECAPPED

They can certainly try. They are likely denying coverage, claiming lack of consent from the owner of the vehicle (the boss). Did the boss know your friend was going to take the vehicle fishing, or did he only lend it to him for business use?

Also, there is the issue of implied consent. Did the boss in the past ever consent to after-hours use of the vehicle? If so, then your friend may have had implied consent, even though he did not have actual consent on this occasion.

You are most likely in for a nightmare of litigation before it is determined who should pay for the injuries. It may be the boss's insurance or your own vehicle insurance under section D of your policy (if you have a car) that ultimately has to pay the claim. Section D is used in cases where there is no other available insurance. If there is no section D or other insurance available, the Facility Association may have to pay out the compensation. Good luck.

(My thanks to Wayne MacDonald at Royal & Sunalliance for his comments.)

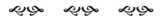

DEAR LISA

Recently I was in an accident and my car was hit from behind. The adjuster from the other driver's insurance company wants to take a statement from me. Should I give her one?

LAWYER-LESS

DEAR LAWYER-LESS

Personal injury lawyers have differing opinions on whether or not their clients should give statements. I, personally, find it helpful to have clients give statements to adjusters, although I like to be present. I once attended a discovery (pre-trial sworn testimony) where the other driver did not have a statement to refresh her memory three years after the accident. When she "recalled" a passenger in the other car who did not exist, her insurance company was forced to pay out the full claim. Statements provided shortly after the accident can eliminate this type of confusion.

Lawyers often prefer to be present for the statement to make sure the adjuster is aware of the client's full injuries and to eliminate any improper questions. Improper questions do not often happen, but I have had to intervene and instruct my client not to answer questions when I thought it might expose them to civil or criminal liability.

DEAR LISA

Someone rear-ended me the other day and I have been trying to get hold of her. I want her to pay for my car repairs (about $575 to replace the bumper), but she is not returning my calls. What if this person doesn't pay the cost of the damage to the car? I don't know the name of her insurance company because I forgot to ask at the time of the accident. I only got her name, phone number and car registration number. What can I do?

POORLY PREPARED

DEAR POORLY PREPARED

The most important information to get from the other driver at an accident is their name, the name of their insurance company and their insurance policy number.

If she refuses to give you this information, she has a duty under the *Motor Vehicle Act* to at least provide you with the following:

- her name;

- address;

- car registration number;

- and to exhibit her driver's licence to you.

You may want to tell her (or her answering machine) that you would really rather not involve a lawyer in the matter. You will be forced to contact one, however, if she does not provide you with her insurance information within seven days of this telephone call.

DEAR LISA

I was in a serious car accident this winter. I was driving in a bad snow storm when my car veered across the road and into a snow bank. Shortly after, an oncoming car hit me. Can I get any compensation from the driver who hit me?

WHITE OUT

DEAR WHITE OUT

Possibly, you may have a claim. You would not, however, be paid for the portion of blame that is yours (if you were found to have some blame). For example, if you caused the emergency situation (by crossing the road), but the other driver still should have taken more care in dealing with the emergency, you may be found 50 percent contributorially negligent (at fault). If the judge, however, considers the other driver had no time to react to avoid impact, then you would probably be held 100 percent responsible. Lighting and road conditions also become factors in deciding what the "reasonable driver" would have done in that unexpected situation.

Problems With Insurance Coverage

DEAR LISA

I was involved in an car accident recently where a car side-swiped me. I was driving and my boyfriend was a passenger. We were both injured. Apparently, the car that hit me was stolen, and I was driving without insurance. Can we get any money for our injuries?

YOUNG BUT LEARNING

DEAR YOUNG

Not for you, unfortunately, since you were driving without insurance.

When you drive without insurance not only do you not have insurance, but you also disqualify yourself from Facility Association funds (which has replaced Judgment Recovery). The Association would help cover these extra costs if there was insurance but not enough to cover all your injuries. The Association normally covers people if there is no other insurance available, unless the lack of insurance is the injured person's fault.

Your boyfriend, however, may have insurance coverage if he or his parents (if he lives at home) have car insurance on their own vehicle (under section D of the policy). Even though your boyfriend's car was not involved in the accident, his policy still covers him in these types of situations when there is no insurance.

If he does not have his own car insurance policy, the Facility Association would pay him compensation up to a maximum of $200,000 since the lack of insurance on the two cars in the accident was not his fault.

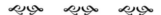

DEAR LISA

I had an injury in a car accident almost four years ago. My own insurance company under section B of my policy has paid for my physiotherapy and shoulder injections, which I still require. The insurance adjuster has told me they are going to cut me off at the 4-year mark. Can they do that?

STILL AILING

DEAR AILING

There is a 4-year time limitation on treatment found in section B of your car insurance policy. Nonetheless, you may be able to successfully sue to reinstate some of the coverage beyond the four years. The courts consider whether your doctor identified a course of treatment before the 4-year limitation, even though the treatment may extend past the four years. If this is the case, the insurance company may have to continue to pay for these specific treatments.

Car Accident Fault Issues

DEAR LISA

I recently rear-ended someone in a very minor car accident. Normally, I don't think he would have been injured, but apparently he has arthritis in his neck which was made much worse after the accident. Will my insurance company still have to fully compensate him if he is more easily hurt than the average person?

KEEPING A LOOK OUT

DEAR LOOK OUT

Yes. The person at fault takes her victim as she finds them. The "thin skull doctrine" states that if you hit someone who happens to have a thin skull, you are still responsible for all of their injuries no matter how extensive and unforeseeable. Your insurance company, however, only has to compensate this person back to their pre-accident status, not back to perfect health (since he already had arthritis).

DEAR LISA

My daughter and I were recently in a rear-ender. We were waiting at a stop sign behind another car when a third car slammed into us. This impact in turn drove us into the car ahead. My husband thinks that we may still be at fault because we hit the car in front of us. Are we at fault?

DOUBLE WHIPLASH

DEAR DOUBLE WHIPLASH

In a rear-ender, the car behind is normally at fault except in your case where your vehicle was not moving, unless you were bumper to bumper, too close to the car in front of you, in which case you may be found partially responsible. Assuming you were not parked too close, the car behind will be responsible for all the damages.

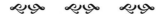

DEAR LISA

I have a friend who refuses to wear a seatbelt while driving in my car. Can she sue me for injuries if she is in an accident with me?

FRUSTRATED DRIVER

DEAR FRUSTRATED DRIVER

Yes. If you caused the accident, she can sue you for her injuries. If her injuries, though, are more severe because she was not wearing a seatbelt, her claim would be discounted accordingly. Compensation is often discounted by 10 to 25 percent for people who do not wear seatbelts.

DEAR LISA

I was just in a car accident. The driver who hit me was at fault and has no car insurance. My neck and back are sprained. Can I get any money to compensate me?

OUT OF LUCK

DEAR OUT OF LUCK

Yes. Your own car insurance (under section D of your policy) should give you money for your injuries and damage to your car. There is often a $250 deductible you pay for the car damage and no deductible for your injury claim. Your insurance rates should not go up if you make such a claim under section D. Call your insurance company immediately.

DEAR LISA

I was in a car accident at the Halifax rotary last week. I was travelling inside the rotary and was struck by a car entering it. Who is at fault? Can I make a claim for this headache I have now?

ROTARY PSYCHIC DRIVING

DEAR ROTARY PSYCHIC

Under the *Motor Vehicle Act* both parties have a duty to stop for any on-coming traffic whether you are already in the rotary or entering it.

Accidents at the rotary often have their liability split 50-50. The facts are usually hard to determine in terms of who had the right of way.

Even if liability is split and you are found 50 percent at fault, you can still make a claim. Your settlement, though, would be reduced by 50 percent.

Disability Insurance

DEAR LISA

I bought life and disability insurance on my mortgage about five years ago. I have recently been diagnosed with lung cancer and the insurance company is refusing to pay the disability part of the claim. I have been off work since last summer. They say because I didn't declare a scope done to my knee for arthritis when I filled out the insurance application, I am disqualified. I forgot to tell the insurance company about my knee because it wasn't very serious and I didn't lose any work. Can they refuse the claim? I am on disability due to lung cancer, not because of my knee.

HINDSIGHT'S 20/20

DEAR HINDSIGHT

To win, the insurance company must show your knee problem was so important they would never have given you the disability coverage in the first place. They have to show that your lack of disclosure was so important that it went to the "root of the contract" allowing them to void it.

If your doctor confirms that your knee – at the time you bought the policy – probably would not have caused you further troubles, you may succeed at trial. A judge decides whether there would have been a disability policy at all or whether there would have been one but with an exclusion for any knee related disabilities. If you can show on a balance of probabilities there would have been a policy – even with an exclusion for your knee – the insurance company will have to pay.

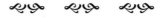

Dog Bites

DEAR LISA

Can I be sued because my dog, Lupine, bit a child when I was walking at Point Pleasant Park?

HOUNDED

DEAR HOUNDED

Yes, you could be sued. If you have house insurance, however, a standard policy will cover your negligent actions (and your dog's bad acts), even if you were in Point Pleasant Park when it happened.

You also should know about the "one bite rule." Your insurance company may not have to pay damages if your dog has not bitten anyone before. If your dog has bitten someone before and you knew about it, your insurance company will likely have to pay. If this happens, your insurance company may get rid of you if you do not get rid of your dog.

Civil Assault

DEAR LISA

I was at one of the pubs downtown and was thrown out by the bouncers. When I came to on the sidewalk, my arm was broken. I passed out when they put a choke-hold on me in the bar. Who can I sue?

CASTING ABOUT FOR ANSWERS

DEAR CASTING

Owners of property are allowed to use "reasonable force" to remove trespassers, that is, people who have been asked to leave and refuse to do so. What is "reasonable" is usually what the trial judge must decide, considering all the circumstances. If you have been asked to leave and do not go immediately, you run the risk of injury. The courts may not compensate you for injury if they deem the force to have been reasonable.

If you were very drunk, very aggressive and/or attacking others, this would make the pub's actions look more reasonable. Other cases with similar facts that have gone to trial have been both won and lost. If you can successfully show that you were not aggressive and/or not resisting their requests to leave the bar, you have a better chance of being successful.

In terms of your damages, in a recent Nova Scotian case, the plaintiff was evicted from a bar and was awarded $20,000 for a badly broken arm.

DEAR LISA

Is there a difference between the terms "assault" and "battery" or do they mean the same thing?

WORD SMITHING

DEAR SMITHING

The common law makes a distinction between the two. Assault is defined as the "intention to create a fear of imminent harm." Assault can be verbal harm: "I'm going to blow up your house." Or, for example, if you take a swing at a person and miss, this is also an assault because a fear of harm was created. The criminal law calls this uttering threats.

Actually landing the punch, though, the common law calls a battery. The *Criminal Code* calls this "assault" (applying force without consent).

Common law is private judge-made law that has developed over centuries. Common law offences are sued between private individuals. Criminal law is public law and prosecuted by the state.

Problem neighbours

6

Real Estate and Problem Neighours

Deeds

DEAR LISA
    I am buying my first piece of land. How exactly does a deed transfer?
                      PUZZLED

DEAR PUZZLED
    A deed is made up of a property description and a cover sheet. The only part of a deed document that technically changes hands, that is, has continuity from one buyer to the next, is the property description, also

known as Schedule A. The property description is the metes and bounds description that states where the land is located and how large the lot is.

With each sale of the land, the seller's lawyer drafts a new cover page for the property description. The new cover page designates the seller of the land as the "grantor" and the buyer as the "grantee." The cover page and the property description (and an affidavit of marital status) form what we call the deed.

DEAR LISA

I just found out that the deed to my cottage was never registered at the Registry of Deeds. Does this affect my ownership of the property?

CLEANING OUT THE CUPBOARDS

DEAR CLEANING

Immediately file the deed at the Registry of Deeds. You may then want to have a title search done to be sure you still have clear title to the cottage. Since your deed was not filed at the Registry, you have not given notice to the world that you own the land. Someone else may have bought the same piece of land after you. If they did not know you had bought it already, they would have the best claim to the land since they have not only a deed but one registered in time before yours. You would have a fraud claim against the original seller of the cottage for selling the same land twice, but you would not have the cottage.

Land Boundary Disputes

DEAR LISA

My neighbour and I have had a long-time dispute about who owns the oak tree in our back yard. Do we contact a lawyer to determine the exact boundaries of our properties?

THE HATFIELDS AND MCCOYS

DEAR HATFIELDS AND MCCOYS

You actually need to contact a land surveyor to determine where your boundaries are. The land surveyor will draw up the property description (Schedule A) based on the property descriptions available at the Registry of Deeds and the landmarks still visible on the ground. Perhaps you and your neighbour can share this cost which can be a couple thousand dollars. If necessary, your lawyer could draft a new deed for you and your neighbour to confirm the new boundaries.

DEAR LISA

Is there any difference between an easement and a right-of-way? I want to ask my neighbour for the right to park my car on part of his driveway.

ILL AT EASE

DEAR AT EASE

A right-of-way is one type of easement. In this case, ask your neighbour for a right-of-way (easement) to use his driveway. This easement should be drawn up by a lawyer and registered at the Registry of Deeds. If your neighbour has a bank mortgage, his bank should also provide a partial release of the mortgage on the easement. This partial release is also filed at the Registry and allows the easement granted to be unaffected by any foreclosure on your neighbour's property.

Real Estate Fees

DEAR LISA

Why do lawyers charge so much for a real estate purchase? We just bought our first home and our lawyer charged us $600 for the legal fees.

FEELING THE NEW HOME PINCH

DEAR FEELING THE PINCH

If it is any consolation, in England the solicitors charge 1 percent of the purchase price. This would mean $1,000 in legal fees for a $100,000 house, or $1,500 for a $150,000 house. From a lawyer's point of view, the sliding scale makes more sense because we insure good title to the property. If there is a recorded judgment or a break in title that makes it difficult for you to sell your house in the future, your lawyer insures your loss. Therefore, a flat fee of $600 – no matter how expensive your house – is really quite a deal.

Now that you feel so much better, here is what you usually get for your money:

- If you have a mortgage, these documents are ordered and completed;
- Closing adjustments such as oil costs and property taxes are calculated;
- Tax certificate is ordered from the municipality to confirm taxes owed by the seller;
- Deed transfer documents are prepared and registered with the municipality;
- Search on title reviewed and a certificate of good and marketable title provided;
- The deed, any mortgage releases and/or declarations are registered.

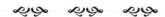

Problem Neighbours

DEAR LISA

Can I sue my neighbours because their dog barks all night?
TIRED AND DISGRUNTLED

DEAR TIRED

You can, but I don't recommend it. You may sue your neighbour for "nuisance," but the legal costs will likely outweigh any money you may receive from the court. A simpler solution is to call your local dog patrol (in Halifax 468-9219) and have the officer give your neighbour a ticket for allowing the dog to bark to the extent that it "persistently disturbs the quiet" of your neighbourhood (HRM By-Law D100, s.11(1)(d)). The ticket is usually $100 for a first offence.

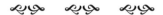

DEAR LISA

My neighbour clear-cut all the trees on his land which were directly next to the trees on my land. After he cut his trees down, the trees on my land have started to blow over because they didn't have any wind protection. Now, I also have a problem with erosion since the trees have been uprooted. What can I do?

WIND BLOWN

DEAR WIND BLOWN

Your neighbour is not allowed to "unreasonably and substantially interfere with the use and enjoyment" of your land. Your neighbour may have committed the tort of nuisance. (A tort is a civil wrongdoing, e.g. trespass, battery or defamation). To prove nuisance, the courts will weigh your neighbour's interest in clear-cutting (is it reasonable or not) with the effect it had on your land. The more substantial the damage to your land, the more likely the court will find the interference unreasonable.

You do not need to prove that your neighbour acted intentionally or negligently when he interfered with your land, just that there was interference. Furthermore, you do not need to prove the damage to your land was caused directly by his actions (e.g. the neighbour cutting your trees down). It is enough that the damage was caused indirectly by him, as it was in this case. Therefore, while your neighbour may not have meant to harm your land, he can still be found liable.

*Present this page to Teryl Scott, Lawyers inc. for a
one-time complimentary power of attorney.*

7

Wills/Estates

Power of Attorney

DEAR LISA

Do I need a power of attorney for my aging mother? What happens if
she has a stroke and she can't manage her affairs?

BEGINNING TO WORRY

DEAR BEGINNING TO WORRY

Every adult should have a power of attorney. An enduring power of
attorney is helpful if your mother, in this case, becomes incapacitated and

can no longer make financial decisions. Your mother must be of sound mind to sign the power of attorney. The cost of a power of attorney is relatively inexpensive – it can be in the $150 range (or free if you bring page 95 to my firm). If she does not have one and your mother has a stroke, you would have to apply to the court for a guardianship order. These are very expensive and would cost you thousands of dollars in legal fees.

Be sure your power of attorney is enduring. If not, the power of attorney will become void upon her incapacity. Non-enduring powers of attorney are used in situations where one party wants another to handle their affairs during their absence. For example, a specific power of attorney could give legal authority to a friend to sign a deed for a real-estate transaction if you were going to be away. The specific power of attorney is written in such a way to restrict its use to this purpose only.

DEAR LISA

My brother has power of attorney as well as being co-executor of our mother's estate. She has Alzheimer disease and lives in a nursing home. Can he make any changes to her will?

SIBLING CURIOSITY

DEAR CURIOSITY

No. Your mother must be of sound mind to make changes to her will. These changes must be made by her, personally, not through a power of attorney. If your mother made her will and then became incapacitated mentally, the will can no longer be changed and it permanently becomes her "last will and testament."

DEAR LISA

I have been given power of attorney over my uncle's affairs. He recently died and the will appoints my brother as executor. Who deals with his bank accounts until the will is probated, me as power of attorney or him as executor?

POWER OF ATTORNEY

DEAR POWER OF ATTORNEY

Upon your uncle's death, the power of attorney terminates. Your brother, as executor/personal representative, immediately has the power to take over your uncle's financial affairs. Banks usually require a copy of the will and a death certificate to allow funds to be released to the personal representative for funeral expenses, etc.

Guardianship

DEAR LISA

My 11-year-old son just received a gift of $80,000 from his grandfather's estate. His grandfather also left him $200,000 in trust which he can have when he turns 19 years old. My son is threatening to buy all kinds of toys and CDs in Walmart with the $80,000. I, of course, do not want this to happen. Can I control that money for him until he is older and more responsible?

KNOWING MY SON

DEAR KNOWING

The Public Trustee has jurisdiction over your child's funds since they come from the grandfather's estate. To protect yourself from your son's discontentment when he turns the age of majority, you may want to have the Public Trustee manage the funds. If you want to control these funds for him, you have to make an application to the court to have yourself declared the financial guardian of your child. You may want to avoid Walmart before then.

DEAR LISA

Do I have the final say over who becomes the guardian of my children when I die?

WILL POWER

DEAR WILL POWER

No. The courts have the final say. Judges, though, will only become involved if someone objects to the guardian appointed in your will. If a judge concludes your guardian will not take care of the best interests of the children, she will appoint someone else. The courts, however, seriously consider the wishes of a deceased parent.

DEAR LISA

My mother, who is a widow, had a stroke six months ago. Unfortunately, she didn't give me a power of attorney prior to her incapacity. I now have to sell her house. What can I do?

FEELING THE BURDEN

DEAR FEELING THE BURDEN

Since there is no power of attorney, you will have to make an application to the court to have yourself (or someone else) declared her guardian. The process is quite involved and requires, among other things, two doctors' certificates of incapacity, a bond to protect the estate, and at least two court appearances. When you have the guardianship order, you can then sign a deed on your mother's behalf to sell her home. The guardian is a trustee and must, of course, at all times act in her best interests.

Executor's (Personal Representative's) Duties in a Will

DEAR LISA

Can I appoint an executor who does not live in the province?

ALONE IN THE PROVINCE

DEAR ALONE

Yes, you can appoint an out-of-province executor/personal representative. There are, however, amendments to the *Probate Act* that now affect out-of-province appointments. You should indicate in your will that your personal representative (as executors are known under the amendments) does not have to post a bond to carry out his or her duties, unless, of course, you want this added security feature imposed on your representative. Before these recent amendments, out-of-province executors were not required to post a security bond to handle the deceased person's affairs.

DEAR LISA

I am executor of my sister's will and I want to probate it. Do I need a lawyer to do it for me?

LOOKING FOR OPTIONS

DEAR LOOKING FOR OPTIONS

No. You do not necessarily need a lawyer to probate a will. But I would recommend a lawyer because the process is very involved and there are a lot of forms required by Probate Court. If you call Probate Court they will provide you with an information package. We have developed at our firm a personal representative's check list which you can request from me at lisa@terylscott.com.

DEAR LISA

My brother recently died quite suddenly. I am concerned that the executor of my brother's estate, his cousin, will not follow the instructions in my brother's will. What can I do?

STILL IN SHOCK

DEAR IN SHOCK

You have a right to see the will. If the executor/personal representative will not allow you to see it, you can make an application to Probate Court to have the will registered at the probate court and/or make an application to have him removed as personal representative. When the will is registered there, you can view it. Probate Court requires a full accounting of your brother's estate within approximately 18 months of his death. In the end, if you think there has been any improper accounting, you can contest the closing of the will when the "Notice to Close" has been sent to the heirs and any interested parties.

DEAR LISA

I just found out I have been appointed the executor of my friend's million dollar estate. Can I refuse to do it? How much will I be paid if I do it?

WEIGHING MY OPTIONS

DEAR WEIGHING

You certainly can refuse to be the executor/personal representative. To do so, you should file a form at Probate Court "renouncing the executorship." If you choose to accept this mission, you will be paid about $30,000 from the estate (1 to 5 percent of the estate, at the discretion of the Registrar of Probate).

DEAR LISA

I was executor for my father's will. He had a fairly large estate so I had everything approved by Probate Court. After probate was closed, a creditor came forward to make a $5,000 claim for a credit-card bill which had not been paid, since I didn't know about it. All the money, though, has been given to the beneficiaries. Do I have to pay the bill myself, since I was the executor?

FEELING THE BURDEN

DEAR FEELING THE BURDEN

No, as executor/personal representative you do not have to pay. One of the purposes of formally "closing probate" is to protect you, as personal representative, from the estate's creditors. The court approved the final distribution of the assets when probate was closed and, therefore, you are shielded from legal liability.

The creditors, however, can chase assets of the estate into the hands of the beneficiaries. Therefore, if you were a beneficiary, the creditor can collect from you for the amount of the assets you received as a beneficiary of your father's estate.

DEAR LISA

I read in your column last week that creditors of an estate can go after the beneficiaries' inheritances even after the will has gone though Probate Court. I was a beneficiary of my mother's life insurance. Can creditors go after these funds?

DIFFERENT ROUTE TO THE SAME PROBLEM

DEAR DIFFERENT

No, the *Insurance Act*, section 198(1), prevents creditors from making claims for these funds if you were listed as a beneficiary on the policy. When a person is directly listed as a policy beneficiary, the insurance funds do not go into the estate and therefore the funds are protected. If, however, your mother listed her estate as the beneficiary and you inherited the funds through her will, then the funds are not protected from creditors.

DEAR LISA

My father-in-law recently passed away, with his wife acting as executor of the will. In the past, my father-in-law had mentioned several times how he had provided money for his grandchild (my daughter) in his will.

My mother-in-law will not discuss the contents of the will with us (we have only asked in passing, not wanting to cause any family problems). What route do I take to get a look at the contents of the will? If, in fact, money has been left for the children, what can I do to make sure my father-in-law's wishes are followed?

WONDERING SON-IN-LAW

DEAR WONDERING

You can make a written request of the executor/personal representative that she "probate the will." When she submits the will to Probate Court for verification, the will can then be viewed by the public since the court keeps a copy of it. If she refuses to probate the will, you can petition probate court to have someone else designated the personal representative. Presumably, this person would then ensure the instructions in your father-in-law's will are followed.

General Will Information

DEAR LISA

I just had my will done last year and I am getting married this fall. Do I need a new will?

READY FOR DEATH AND MARRIAGE

DEAR READY

Yes. Under the *Wills Act*, your old will becomes invalid upon marriage. You must write a new one unless your lawyer put in a "contemplation of marriage" clause in your old will. With this clause, the will continues to be valid after you marry.

If you do not have the clause in your will, you cannot add it to your existing will by creating a codicil (an amendment, which is less expensive than a full will). Unfortunately, you must have a whole new will signed.

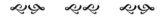

DEAR LISA

I understand wills registered with Probate Court can be viewed by the public. Why is such a personal document made public?

PRIVATELY CONCERNED

DEAR CONCERNED

The registering of wills is a form of public accountability which ensures that the wishes of the deceased person are respected. If you do not want the public to know the value of your estate, you may want to leave your heirs with a specified percentage of your estate instead of an exact dollar amount, although the final accounting when probate is finalized is available for public review.

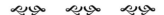

Will Kits

DEAR LISA

Should I get a do-it-yourself "will kit" and do my own will?

LOOKING FOR A DEAL

DEAR LOOKING

I do not recommend it. If you have a very simple will (i.e., you are leaving everything to only one adult), this method may work, but even then there are definitely risks involved. For example, your will will not be valid if the very strict formalities of signing and witnessing it are not followed.

If you have young children, who require a guardian and a trust, I recommend that you pay a lawyer to do this work for you. The cost of a will can range from $100 to $200 (more or less), depending on the complexities involved.

Clear and unambiguous wording in a will is very important. For example, one of my clients wanted her child to receive all the money from her estate "when he marries" instead of when the child turned 19 years old. I could not let her structure the will this way because if her child did not marry, he would never receive the estate.

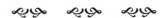

DEAR LISA

Is it necessary to pay a lawyer to validate your will in Nova Scotia if you use a do-it-yourself kit?

ORDERING AFFAIRS

DEAR ORDERING

No. Lawyers are not needed to validate (or witness) a will whether it is drafted by a lawyer or done from a kit. Two witnesses of the testator's (the person creating the will) signature are required. Witnesses or their spouses should not be beneficiaries. If a witness signs the will and is also a beneficiary, the gift to the witness is either forfeited or the person cannot be used as a witness. Failure to have at least two witnesses invalidates the will.

The witnesses and the testator must also initial each page of the will to show these are original pages to the document. Both witnesses must be present at the same time to witness the testator's signature. If any of these formalities are missing, the will, or parts of it, are invalid.

If you use the kit, you should at least have a lawyer review it to determine your intentions are clear and the formalities properly completed. The rules for drafting and interpreting wills can be complex.

Living Wills

DEAR LISA

What is a living will?

LOOKING TO AVOID DEATH

DEAR LOOKING

A living will contains your wishes for medical treatment in the event you become terminally ill or persistently unconscious and unable to provide informed consent to your doctors. The agreement is formalized into a statement signed by you and witnessed. Among other things, this declaration gives guidance to physicians and loved ones on whether you want to be maintained on life support or not. The Legal Information Society of Nova Scotia has useful pamphlets on numerous subjects, including living wills (1-800-665-9779, www.legalinfo.org).

DEAR LISA

My mother recently passed away and left her estate to my brother and me. A couple of months before she died, she added my brother's name to her bank account so that he could manage her banking. Someone told me that the money ($30,000) is his now since it was a joint bank account. Am I entitled to any of it since I am in her will?

THE OTHER CHILD

DEAR OTHER

When joint accounts are set up, there is a "presumption of advancement." This means, in your case, if the money was jointly held between your mother and brother, there is a presumption that the money was meant to "advance" or go to him in the event of her death. To rebut the presumption, you must be able to show that the joint account arrangement was merely a convenience and the money was not intended as a gift to your brother. If all of the money was your mother's, and she did not specifically give it to your brother before she died, you have the right to ask that the money be included in the estate.

DEAR LISA

I just found out I have been cut out of a will. My rich uncle from Trenton, Nova Scotia, had repeatedly told my sister and I that we would inherit a portion of his estate when he died. My uncle had told me he was leaving everything to his partner with the understanding that we would be entitled to our uncle's funds after his partner died.

After my uncle died a few years ago, I met his partner and we didn't get along. I just found out that his partner recently died. Her children and my sister were included in the will but not me. Am I cut out for good?

CUTTING IN

DEAR CUTTING IN

You would have to establish that a "constructive trust" had been set up by your rich uncle with his partner as the trustee. A constructive trust is a trust that the court constructs after the fact. Even though there was no formal written trust at the time your uncle passed on, the court can assume this was your uncle's intention if there is enough evidence. That your sister inherited under the partner's will, and you did not get along with the partner are facts that can be interpreted as intentionally excluding you from the will. You would also have to show that your uncle did not change his mind about this informal trust just before his death.

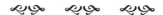

DEAR LISA

I have an estranged daughter: no phone calls, Mother's Day cards, birthday cards or Christmas greetings from her for several years now. We have no communication at all. Do I have to include her in my will? I am a widow in my mid-70s and would like to have my affairs in order.

VERY CONCERNED MOTHER

DEAR VERY CONCERNED

No, you do not have to put her in your will. You may wish to specify in your will why you have not included her. Your daughter may be able to contest the will under the *Testator's Family Maintenance Act* (dependent's relief legislation) if she can show she is a "dependent." Therefore, you will want to provide the court with your reasoning (in the will) and to show you have given it considerable thought.

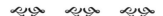

Life Insurance and Wills

DEAR LISA

Should I take out life insurance so that my student loan is paid off when I die? My bank told me my parents would have to pay this debt if my estate could not afford to pay it. I am single and don't have any assets.

DOWN THE GARDEN PATH

DEAR GARDEN PATH

Your bank has given you inaccurate information. Debts that survive death are uncollectable if your estate has no assets. If your estate has value, your debts are paid first before your beneficiaries receive anything. Debts in your name alone would not be transferable to anyone else upon your death unless there was a co-signer involved. In such as case, they would assume the whole debt.

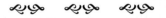

DEAR LISA

Should I designate my children specifically on my life insurance policy, or should I leave it generally to my estate?

GETTING PREPARED

DEAR PREPARED

There are no taxes paid on life insurance proceeds whether left to the estate or received directly by the beneficiaries. Leaving life insurance to your estate is a good strategy if you plan to set up testamentary trusts in your will. Earnings from the investment of the life insurance proceeds will be taxable but could be split among a number of beneficiaries, using testamentary trusts to minimize taxes.

There are two disadvantages when you leave life insurance to your estate:

- The proceeds could be subject to the claims of creditors (i.e., if your estate has any debts, life insurance left to your estate would pay these debts before the remainder can be distributed). On the other hand, sometimes life insurance is left to the estate precisely to pay debts and therefore protect the other assets in the estate.

- The proceeds will be subject to probate fees. When your will goes to Probate Court, the value of your estate is determined and the court charges your estate fees based on the value of the estate. (Over $100,000, the fees are approximately 1.2 percent).

If the disadvantages are significant to you, you could list beneficiaries directly on the policy so the insurance proceeds are not included in the estate.

Nursing Homes

DEAR LISA

My mother has to go into a nursing home. Can the government take her house if she has no money?

PROTECTING MY INHERITANCE

DEAR PROTECTING

No. The government cannot take her house, but she must fill out a Designation of Primary Residence Form. This form must be signed by your mother and pre-date her will. Lawyers can also provide you with the form.

Your mother does not actually designate her house to anyone. The designation just tells Community Services that it has been her main residence for at least two years. After it is signed, they cannot force her to sell the house to pay for her expenses at the nursing home.

You should also know:

- If she sells her home, the money from the sale can be used by Community Services for her care.

- Surrounding land acreage can be included in the designation if it can be regarded as "reasonably contributing to the use and enjoyment of the residence."

- She can designate her home before or after entering the nursing home.

DEAR LISA

How does the government determine if I have enough money to pay for my nursing home costs?

PLANNING AHEAD

DEAR PLANNING AHEAD

The government calculates whether you have the funds to pay for at least 18 months of care. If the value of all your assets and annual income exceeds approximately $45,000, then you pay for the nursing home costs.

When your money runs out, the government takes over the cost of the care.

Be sure you "designate" your home, so that it is not included as an asset.

If you have a spouse who does not need nursing home care, then only 50 percent of your collective assets would be considered by the government for your care.

Intestacies – Dying Without a Will

DEAR LISA

My mother just died without a will. She never married and her abusive common-law husband says that he gets her whole estate. Is that true?

BEREAVED

DEAR BEREAVED

Probably not. Her common-law husband would not get any of her estate as a beneficiary, unless their common-law status had been confirmed with a Domestic Partnership Declaration (see Chapter 3, Common-Law Couples). Under the *Intestate Succession Act*, you (and her other children, if any) receive her entire estate. Had he married her, he would have received a substantial portion of her estate. The amount depends on the size of the estate.

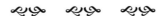

Estate Taxes

DEAR LISA

My grandfather is in his 90s and I expect he will pass on soon. He has over $60,000 in his savings account which I am to inherit when he dies. Will there be taxes payable on these funds?

SPENDER NOT A SAVER

DEAR SPENDER

Estates are only taxed on *income* earned after the date of death (including interest, dividends, and capital gains). The money in your grandfather's savings account would normally be after-tax money and therefore not taxed again upon his death. These funds, though, would be subject to probate fees unless your grandfather adds you jointly to the savings account before he dies.

If you are listed as joint owners on the account, these funds will go directly to you, and not to the estate, thereby avoiding probate fees.

The major tax hit happens upon death (in the absence of a spousal rollover) when the deceased tax payer is deemed to dispose of all his/her assets at fair market value resulting in capital gains (i.e., the increase in the value of the asset is taxed) and RRSPs being deregistered. These gains must all be reported in the final tax return.

DEAR LISA

My sister, father and I are now on the deed to my father's house as joint tenants since my father became a widower a year and a half ago. If he dies, do we have to pay taxes on it and who gets his portion of the house?

AVOIDING A SWIM IN ESTATE TAXES

DEAR AVOIDING A SWIM

Since you both have your names on the deed jointly, his share of the house will go equally to you and your sister when your father dies. The house does not go through his will. If you and your sister later sell the house for greater than the market value at the time the property transferred to the three of you, you will have to pay tax on the capital gains (increased value of the asset).

DEAR LISA

How does a trust work? I have well over a million dollars in my estate. What is the best way to leave money to my children and grandchildren so they pay the least taxes?

PREPARING NOW

DEAR PREPARING

Assuming that you do not wish to transfer any of your assets to your children/grandchildren during your lifetime, the type of trust that may be beneficial is a "testamentary trust." A testamentary trust is a trust that is established in your will. It can be a useful way of distributing funds to individuals on an after-tax basis, taking advantage of lower tax brackets.

A trust created by a will is taxed like a separate/individual taxpayer for income tax purposes. As a separate taxpayer, the trust pays taxes according to its income level for any given year. Trusts are flexible, however, and the income that a trust makes can be taxed at the trust level or in the hands of the beneficiaries.

The "marginal tax rate" is the percentage of taxes you pay on the last dollar you make in any given year. The marginal rates for Nova Scotia for 2002 are approximately as follows:

- The initial $7,500-$30,000 is taxed at 26 percent.

- The next $30,000-$60,000 is taxed at 37 percent.

- The next $60,000-$100,000 is taxed at 43 percent.

- Any remaining money over $100,000 is taxed at 47 percent.

Accordingly, if income from an estate can be taxed in one or more trusts rather than added to the existing income of the heir/beneficiary, substantial tax savings can be achieved. The goal is to have the estate's wealth spread over one or more trusts to allow the trusts' incomes to fit in low tax brackets. Placing the estate into smaller trusts (and taxing it there) also prevents your heir's overall income from being pushed into the next tax bracket.

For example, if funds are not protected by a trust and your child already has an existing income at the top tax bracket, and a further $30,000 (i.e., from interest earned on the inheritance) is added to her income, this

$30,000 would also be taxed at the top tax bracket. Your child would take home only $15,900 (47% or $14,100 paid in taxes) of the $30,000.

If the income was earned through a testamentary trust and taxed in the trust, and these funds are distributed to the same beneficiary, there would be $24,150 after-tax dollars available for distribution to her. (The funds would be taxed in trust at the lowest tax bracket – the first $7,500 being tax free, the remaining funds being taxed at a 26 percent.) Total taxes payable to the government on the $30,000 would be only $5,850 instead of $14,100 – a saving of $8,250 per year. A professionally prepared will that establishes one or more testamentary trusts can be a valuable estate planning tool.

(My thanks to Boyd Hunter, CA, CFP, at Hunter & Belgrave Chartered Accountants, for his extensive comments.)

8

More Questions You Couldn't Afford to Ask

DEAR LISA
How long does it take to become a lawyer?

PAPERCHASED

DEAR PAPERCHASED
Law school takes three years. To get into law school, you must write the Law School Admissions Test (LSAT). You also normally must have a university degree, unless you are a mature student, Nova Scotian Black or

Mi'kmaq when this requirement is sometimes waived. Part-time studies are available.

When you finish law school, you have to apprentice (called articling) for one year with a lawyer, write bar exams, and then you are part of the club!

DEAR LISA

How do I become a paralegal?

HIGH SCHOOL GRAD

DEAR GRAD

There is not yet any formal paralegal association that governs paralegals, although the Nova Scotia Barristers' Society is currently considering defining their role. There are, however, many trade schools that offer certificate or diploma paralegal programs. For example, CAC Career College has a paralegal program in Lower Sackville (I assisted in developing their program). The University College of Cape Breton has a paralegal degree program. The programs can range from one to three years. You normally need a grade 12 education or equivalent to enter the program.

Paralegals can assist with almost all aspects of a legal practice including drafting legal documents, legal research, interviewing witnesses, and requesting medical reports for personal injury claims. They are not allowed to provide legal advice or represent clients in court.

DEAR LISA

I am not very happy with my lawyer. He never returns my calls. I have made more than 30 calls in the last month and he has not contacted me in return. What can I do?

NEGLECTED CLIENT

DEAR NEGLECTED

It is important for you to feel you can reasonably communicate with your lawyer. Is he away on vacation? Assuming he is not, here are some suggestions:

- Sometimes a letter mailed or dropped off to the lawyer (keep a copy for yourself) will work when phone messages do not.

- Tell his secretary you must have a reply by the end of the week or you will be forced to consider having another lawyer take over handling the file.

- As a last resort, you can contact the Barristers' Society to file a written complaint. If you choose this option, remember that you will be terminating your relationship with your lawyer.

Generally, give your lawyer a couple of days to return your calls since many are in court or discoveries, and it is often not possible to return calls earlier.

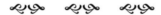

DEAR LISA

I've been in court a few times and the judges seemed fairly young (middle-aged). How many years do they practice law before becoming judges? What is their pay scale?

VIEW FROM THE PEW

DEAR VIEW

It takes a minimum of 10 years at the bar as a lawyer to become a judge. The pay varies depending on the level of the judge, but as of April 1, 2001, provincial court judges make $144,000 (tribunal decision, *Provincial Court Act*).

DEAR LISA

I enjoy reading your column every week, but do people really ask you those questions?

SKEPTIC

DEAR SKEPTIC

Truth really is stranger than fiction. Questions normally come from readers and clients in my practice, with their consent. The more "unique" fact situations are normally real situations (who can think these things up?).

For example, the "doggie custody" question is from a reader, while two different clients recently asked me if their power of attorney continues to be effective after they die, which I combined into one question.

Glossary

Absolute discharge: A criminal sentence imposed by the judge where there is no criminal conviction. For example, when a person is asked on an employment application if they have a criminal conviction, they can respond "no." Technically there is a finding of guilt entered on the court record but not a conviction.

Affidavit: Written, sworn evidence produced during the course of legal proceedings. A judge can **waive** the requirement at trial to give verbal evidence, if it is instead provided in the form of this **sworn** statement.

Application: Also referred to as a court application. There are many types of applications but they fall into three categories: (1) those that start court proceedings (e.g., a family court application); (2) those that deal with an issue before the final and full hearing, also called an "interim application" (e.g., interim spousal support is when support is ordered by a judge on a temporary basis until the final judge can decide what should be paid; and (3) those that involve a review of an existing order.

Assault: Two meanings: (1) The private law between individuals (**civil law**) defines this as a threat of imminent harm. (2) The criminal law defines it as intentional unwanted physical contact, like hitting.

Balance of probabilities: The **civil** standard used by judges or juries to determine whether a defendant is **liable** for **damages** or other remedies.

Battery: Intentional unwanted physical contact such as hitting which is sued privately between individuals. A kind of **tort**. The criminal law calls it **assault**.

Beyond a reasonable doubt: How sure a judge or jury must be that the accused is guilty of a criminal offence. The term is not specifically defined as a percentage since its meaning varies slightly from person to person. The standard for liability in civil offences is less and is defined as a **balance of probabilities**.

Cause of action: The right to sue which has been recognized by the courts as a legal wrong deserving of compensation. Being impolite, for example, has no cause of action. The courts have refused to grant compensation for these types of wrongs. Walking on the neighbour's grass, however, has been recognized as a legal wrong called **trespass**.

Civil law: Private law practiced in Quebec which is codified, meaning consolidated, into a book (and not simply based on judge-made decisions over time). Quebec is the only province in Canada that has this kind of law which is based on the French Civil Code. Private law in English Canada is called **common law** but is also referred to as civil proceedings, although it is not codified.

Commissioner of oaths: A non-lawyer appointed to administer an oath and **to swear** (see **sworn**) documents that remain within the province.

Common law: Two meanings: (1) Judge-made law that creates and defines a body of law through court decisions over time. For example, the law of **trespass** is found by piecing together many court decisions. There is no statute in Nova Scotia defining and awarding compensation for **tort** of **trespass**. (2) To live together unmarried (although romantically) with another person for at least one year, although this time can vary according to the statute that governs the activity (i.e., pension division, entitlement under wills, etc.).

Conditional discharge: A sentence given in criminal matters which allows a guilty person – after completing their conditions set by the court – to receive an **absolute discharge**.

Conditional sentence: A sentence that can be served "in the community" (e.g., they must remain in their house with a curfew). If the convicted person does not obey the conditions of the sentence, he or she can be ordered to spend the rest of the sentence in prison.

Contingency fee agreement: A contract, usually with a personal injury lawyer, that allows the payment of legal fees to be deferred until the claim is settled or court ordered. The lawyer takes a certain percentage of the settled or awarded sum. Should the lawyer be unable to achieve a settlement or loses at trial, no legal fee is owed by the client to the lawyer.

Contract: A contract must have three components before it is considered a contract: (1) An *offer* of some kind with (2) *acceptance* by the other party with a (3) *value* of some sort flowing between the parties (e.g., A free promise to shovel the neighbour's walkway by Friday is not a contract. If one is paid $5 to do it, then it becomes a binding contract.)

Court application: See Application.

Crown attorney: Also referred to as the "Crown." The Crown attorney is the lawyer who represents the government when involved in court proceedings. In the U.S. this person is referred to as the District Attorney.

Custody: (1) Joint custody entitles parents to share equally in the major decisions of the children's lives such as religious instruction, schooling, health. Both parents are presumed to have joint custody unless there is a court order that says otherwise. This term is contrasted with (2) sole custody, which gives this power entirely to one of the parents. Neither of these terms affects the day to day access either parent has with the children, except where it may touch upon a major decision. For example, if the access parent was not religious, but the sole custodian was, the access parent would be obligated to take the child/ren to church. See also **shared custody**, and **primary care and control**.

Damages: Two meanings: (1) Injury or harm to a party. ("What are your damages?" meaning injuries or losses.) (2) Compensation awarded by the court. ("The court awarded $10,000 in damages.")

Day-to-day care and control: See **primary care and control**.

Deductible: The amount payable out of pocket by a person making an insurance claim and then the remainder is paid by the insurance company.

Defamation: Two kinds: (1) Libel: lowering a person's character in the eyes of the public using falsely written words (e.g., newspaper publishing a false story). (2) Slander: lowering a person's character in the eyes of the public with false verbal words (e.g., giving a false public speech about another).

Discoveries: Pre-trial sworn testimony. It is usually taken at one of the lawyers' board-rooms in the presence of a court clerk who tape-records the session. It is a "fishing expedition" for both lawyers who each interview the other party. This process assists in removing all surprises from the upcoming trial which promotes settlement (i.e., knowing the strengths and weaknesses of each other's cases).

Docket appearance: A short appointment in front of a judge to book a full hearing date. The term is often associated with family or provincial court

Duty counsel: A lawyer paid by the province who is available 24 hours per day to provide temporary legal advice over the telephone for criminal matters. The lawyer is available regardless of income level, unlike legal aid lawyers who are only available to people with low incomes.

Execution order: The order required by the sheriff to collect on a successful judgment at court. When the case is won, the judge gives a "judgment order" which is then converted into an "execution order." The execution order states in it the terms of the garnishment etc. (see **garnish**). The **Small Claims Court** sends out an execution order when the successful party sends them the judgment.

Garnish a wage: The court or the Maintenance Enforcement Program can order that funds be deducted from a person's wages or from other sources. Also see **Execution order**.

Guardian ad litem: See **litigation guardian**.

Hybrid offence: An offence that can be classified as a **summary offence** or a more serious **indictable offence**. The **Crown** has the final decision on which way the charges will proceed.

Indictable offence: A more serious *Criminal Code* offence: the maximum punishment is up to life imprisonment for certain offences. For more serious indictable offences, criminal procedures like **preliminary hearings** and jury trials are often available.

Interim application: See **application**.

Interim order: See **application**.

Intestate: To die without a will or with a will that fails to provide for certain situations that occur.

Irrevocable direction to pay: A document signed by a client of a lawyer directing the lawyer to pay to a third-party (often a creditor) money from a settlement the lawyer is handling on behalf of the client. This document acts like a loan guarantee since the creditor will be paid before any money is paid to the client. Since it is "irrevocable," the lawyer is obligated to pay the funds to the creditor even if the client changes her mind.

Issue or court issued: Any document that is court stamped as being received by the court.

Joint custody: See **custody**.

Judgment: When a party is successful at court, the court issues an order which is also called a judgment. If applicable, judgments can be registered at the Registry of Deeds. If the unsuccessful party ever buys or sells real estate, they would have to pay out the judgment before the sale could be completed. Also see **Execution order**.

Judicial stay: See **stay**.

Jurisdiction: Usually refers to the legal or physical limitations of a court. For example, some of jurisdictional limitations of the **Small Claims Court** of Halifax are: (1) only claims within Halifax Regional Municipality can (usually) be heard by the court; (2) only claims under $10,000 can be heard, which is stipulated by its statute.

Liable: To be responsible or at fault for **civil** wrong. One is "liable for **damages**." The criminal law calls it being "guilty" of a crime.

Libel: See **defamation**.

Litigation guardian: All children under the age of 19 must have appointed a guardian to assist them with court proceedings. This person is usually a parent, although it need not be.

Notwithstanding: Despite.

Nuisance (private): To interfere with a neighbour's use and enjoyment of their land in an unreasonable and substantial way. It is a **tort** or legal **cause of action** that allows one to sue for money or an injunction (an order to stop noise, for example).

Orderly Payment of Debts Program: A government program offered by Service Nova Scotia and Municipal Relations (1-800-670-4357) which allows a person to consolidate debt and to pay it back within five years with a low interest rate of 5 percent. The program also protects the person from having their wages garnished.

Organizational pre-trial: A meeting with the trial judge – usually months before the trial – to organize how many witnesses will be called and any important evidence or other procedural motions that need to be managed. The meeting usually clarifies and better focuses the issues to be resolved at trial.

Personal service: See **service**.

Preliminary hearing: Only available for more serious criminal offences. It is like a mini-hearing before the full trial. The Crown must present to a judge evidence on each of the elements of the offence before a judge will allow the charges to go to a full trial. It is also an opportunity for defence counsel to assess the strength of the Crown's case. The Crown, though, does not have to present the full case at this time.

Primary care and control: Regardless of which parent may have joint or sole **custody**, one of them is usually designated the parent who has primary care and control. This is normally the person who spends the most time with the children. That parent would take care of selecting the family doctor and dentist, etc. for the children.

Probate Court: The court where wills are proven valid and estate matters are administered.

Quit claim deed: A deed that transfers property but does not guarantee any good and marketable title. The owner gives over or "quits" any interest they have in the property to the new owner. The new owner takes the land "as is, where is." There-fore, there may be others who claim an interest in the land, or liens attaching to the land that could make the land difficult to resell. See **Warranty deed**.

Restitution: The repayment of money to a victim of a crime. For example, a person guilty of damaging a vehicle may be ordered to pay restitution to the owner. This amount would be the cost of the repairs.

Service: The **Small Claims Court** requires personal service, unless otherwise dictated by the court. The defendant, therefore, must receive notice of the upcoming court date by having the papers personally served on her or him. In this court, service can be done by the claimant or another person but an affidavit should be **sworn** by the server that it was served.

Settlement oriented pre-trial: A meeting with a judge who is not the trial judge – usually months before the trial – to reduce the contested issues or to attempt a full settlement. Matters discussed at the settlement hearing are not to be repeated to the trial judge by either party (while on the witness stand, for example). All references to the settlement discussions are deleted from the court file if the matter goes to trial.

Shared custody: Both parents significantly share the **day to day care and control** of the children. For example, each parent has the children for 50 percent of the week.

Slander: See **defamation**.

Small Claims Court: A court where certain claims for less than $10,000 can be heard (soon to be increased to $15,000). Lawyers are not necessary. Also, the cost of the lawyer's fees on the winning side cannot be awarded against the defeated party.

Sole custody: See **Custody**.

Split custody: Each parent takes **custody** of a child (if there are two children for example).

Stay: There are two kinds of stays: (1) The **Crown attorney** can stay a matter which means to suspend the criminal proceedings against an accused until a future date. (2) A judge can order a stay (judicial stay), permanently stopping a criminal proceeding. The accused may go free and there is neither a finding of guilt nor innocence.

Subpoena: A document issued by the court requiring a witness (and/or documents) to attend court. This document differs from a **summons**. Failure to attend court after being personally served a subpoena can result in a warrant being issued for the witness's arrest.

Subsequent: Following; coming later in time; after.

Summary offence: A less serious *Criminal Code* offence: the maximum fine is $2,000 and the maximum jail time is six months (s.787(1)) to 18 months for certain offences. No **preliminary hearing** or jury is available for these offences.

Summons: A document which is **issued** by the court and requires a person who is charged with an offence to attend court. This document differs from a **subpoena**. Failure to attend court after being personally **served** a summons can result in a warrant being issued for the accused's arrest.

Sworn or to swear: Two meanings: (1) A form of verbal release or venting after a bad day in court; (2) To sign a document in the presence of a lawyer or **commissioner of oaths**.

Tort: A legal wrong which is sued between private individuals (the government, for example, is not normally involved as a party).

Trespass: To unlawfully enter onto or walk across another's property.

Waiver: To abandon or give up a legal right or opportunity, such as waiving one's right to a lawyer.

Warranty: A warranty is a promise that a fact is true and is relied upon in a contract. A breach of warranty would allow **damages** to be paid to the party who relied on it.

Warranty deed: A deed that guarantees to a buyer good and marketable title to real estate (i.e., that there are no liens or judgments and that the owner in fact is the only owner of the property). This kind of deed helps ensure good resale value of the land. See **quit claim deed**.

Index